The Way It Was

How It Was

By

Elwood Ware

authorHOUSE™

1663 LIBERTY DRIVE, SUITE 200
BLOOMINGTON, INDIANA 47403
(800) 839-8640
WWW.AUTHORHOUSE.COM

First published by AuthorHouse 11/08/04

ISBN: 1-4107-4318-7 (e)
ISBN: 1-4184-5206-8 (sc)

This book is printed on acid-free paper.

Printed in the United States of America
Bloomington, Indiana

Special thanks go to the people who helped make this book possible: My mother Nettie Ware for the history of the story. My sister Ann Ware-Lokey. My daughter Porsche Ware for assisting me. My friend Anita Horne for assisting me with whatever was needed to be done.

1. txt

North Carolina, 1852. The son of a slave, the first generation of the free Jankenses – although he was born free, slavery was still very much existent – he lived and felt as if he was a slave himself. Unpleasant life conditions caused a continuous daily struggle for Tom Jankens, his wife Maggie and their three children: fifteen-year-old son Luther, their twelve-year-old son Harry, and their ten-year-old daughter Moellen.

The Jankens family lived on a tobacco plantation where you worked the fields as long as there was light to see.

An opportunity for a better life would be welcomed, and then it happened. Rumors spread around the valley that white men were in the area looking for black families to move across the country to a better life and live in a bigger house, with lots of food, and the money was so plentiful for all over the valley – all you have to do is pick it.

"Tom, you are being foolish. Mr. Benson will never let us go."

"Maggie, we are not slaves. We are free people to live here if we wish."

"Tom, this life is all we know."

"Maggie, there are possibilities out there and we have to go for it."

"Ok, Tom, but he will try to stop us."

"You can pick as many sacks full per day as you wish."

Tom and Maggie discussed the idea, but fast money overpowered their unschooled and underskilled minds – that motivated them to make the move.

The Jankens family lived on a tobacco plantation. Tom would use a double team of mules in the highly hot and humid bottom land, where he would work all day in the burning, hot, scorching sun without a shirt or shoes – not because he wanted to be half-dressed, it was because he had no shirt or shoes, but the freshly plowed dirt sure felt good to his bare feet.

He knew his family had no food to prepare a meal. When he returned home from a devastating day of work, Tom walked down the road a mile or so to see if he could borrow some cornmeal to see if his wife Maggie could fix a small bite to eat for his family and himself.

On Tom's journey back home, a passing stranger noticed that Tom was in a very sad state of mind. That is when he was introduced to the idea that white men were looking for families to move across the country for a much better life.

Tom took this information into very little thought. He was unsure what he was going to do until he decided to go home through the back way. As he walked up to the back, he found families sitting on the back step eating a little ball from a wild plant called a maypop. That is when Tom made his decision to make the move to Mississippi in search for a better life.

2. txt

The Jankens family joined the wagon train early morning, April 12, 1852, along with some other black families and just two white families.

My name is Moellen Jankens, the third child and the only daughter of the Jankenses. I am ten years old and this is how it happened.

Day one, as we started in the direction of a better life, excitement and joy motivated us and gave us strength and courage to carry on. So far, the white men were nice: they treated us like people.

After a full day of travel, just before sunset, we built a campfire and started to roast a beef shoulder. After supper, there was some music and dancing.

Day two, early light, the journey continued at a slow but constant pace. The chill in the early-spring, late-night air was quite uncomfortable. Along with my baby brother I snuggled between my mother and father for warmth. It was my father who stretched his arm out and wrapped me in tightly, laying on the wagon's bare wooden floor with very little cover. It was impossible to be comfortable, but day after day we continued.

We have now traveled hundreds of miles – trails are beginning to take their tolls. It is now early June. I am admiring the beauty of the wildflowers on the mountainsides. It has been weeks since we have seen any people other than ourselves.

3. txt

The white men's attitudes had changed. We were being yelled at and pushed around. The trails were rough. Most of the time we had to walk and push the wagon through bad spots.

In the late afternoons, the head wagon-master yelled out, "We better make camp. Looks like a bad storm heading this way."

The wagon was pulled to a circle with a canvas pulled across the top for shelter. Within minutes, the winds picks up and started to get stronger and stronger. The trees were laying half to the ground, fire popping, lighting up the area as clear as day. The horses had started to get really restless. A burst of thunder roved through the area with monstrous sounds.

The rain continued into the next day. Mid-afternoon, the trail scout returned to camp with unwelcome news. The trails were flooded and backed up from the river. It would be days before we could move. The canvas had been blown from one of the supply wagons. Most of the food had been rained on. We were now cut down to one small portion per day that was served at dusk.

My father knew that, if the river was flooded, there had to be some wild game trapped in the area, and if he cast a net when the water drops back into the river, it's possible that he could catch some fish. He stripped some bark from a tree and made a net.

Success was granted: two rabbits and fish that were in a run-off stream. For a short time food was plentiful on the fourth day after the storm.

4. txt

Within days the food supply was about gone. Just after a small supper, mama was nursing my baby brother from her breast.

There was a young white couple with a baby, maybe just a few months younger than my baby brother. The baby was crying non-stop. The couple was continuing to stare at my mama. Then the man stood up and came over.

"Ma'am, my wife is not producing enough milk to feed our child. We surely will be obliged if you would allow our baby to nurse from your breast. Our baby probably won't survive the trip if you don't do it."

Mama looked at daddy, then she said, "I don't know about a white baby nursing from a colored woman's breast. That just could cause us more problems than what we already have."

"You have to; our baby will die." Mama gave in and hid out behind a wagon and let the baby nurse from her breast. The scout came riding in hard, stopped at the wagon-master, and said, "Riders are coming this way about two miles out. Fifteen to twenty of them. I can't tell if they are lawmen or outlaws. We better stop and set up as if we are broke down. Get that busted wheel down, take the good one off. Women and children, get over that cliff and keep them children quiet." Half the white men with guns took cover.

Soon the rider rode up and stopped. "I see you are broke down, you need some help?"

"No, we be ok."

The man noticed that the good wheel had wet mud on it and the busted wheel was dry.

5. txt

"Me and my men have been on the trail for days. You think we can share some beans and coffee with you?"

"No, we are running short on food with none to spare. Why don't you men ride on? We will be just fine."

At that time a baby cried out behind the cliff. The man started to get from his horse, and that is when the men behind the trees stepped out with their guns and said, "Mister, you just better ride on like the man said."

The word was out that we would reach our destination within days.

Finally, the trip was over; we have arrived, but to what? Where is the money field? "Mama, can I go pick the money with Papa?"

"Baby, I don't see any money fields." All that was there were fields and fields of cotton.

"Ok, people, we are here. This is the Macket Plantation. Soon, you will meet Mr. Charlie Macket. He will explain everything to you. Here he is now."

"I want to thank you men for another good trip. How many do we have? Nine colored families and two white families. I know you were told that money grows in the field and all you have to do is just pick it. Well, it's true; I have fields of cotton – you will pick it and I will turn it into money. For you white families, I will find special jobs for you."

We were placed in a one-room shack, very much like the one we had left back in North Carolina.

It was weeks after we arrived in Mississippi, days into the cotton-picking season. There was some families that had been on the plantation for generations. Most of the new arrivals had never seen cotton before.

There was an old man and a young boy, possibly around eight years old. I am not sure how long they had been on the plantation. They did not communicate very much with each other. They mostly kept to themselves until they were working the field. The man had lost his right eye for reasons unknown to us. Everybody called him the "one-eye man."

The young boy worked a row of cotton beside the one-eye man, where he was working two rows. The young boy was struggling to keep up, causing him to leave cotton behind.

Mr. Macker would ride his big horse into the field to look over the people's performance. The boy had been warned several times about not leaving cotton behind or he would be whipped. The one-eye man worked hard, barely ever looking up. It was mid-morning, and Mr. Macker road his horse into the field and over to the one-eye man and the boy. Then he dismounted his horse took his pocket knife and cut a heavy cotton stalk, trimmed it up, then called out to the one-eye man, "Old man."

The one-eye man slowly looked up and said, "Yes, sir, Mr. Macker."

"Old man, I have warned this boy about leaving cotton behind."

Then he passed the old man the cotton stalk and said, "I want you to whip that boy; he is leaving too much cotton behind. I said whip him, old man."

The old man took off his cotton sack, took the boy by one of his arms and started to whip him across his back. While the boy was hollering and rolling on the ground, Mr. Macker continued to yell out, "Whip him, whip him, whip him."

After about twenty lashings, Mr. Macker finally said, "That's enough." Mr. Macker then said, "I don't want any cotton left behind by anyone."

Then he mounted his horse and road off. When Mr. Macker got out of range, the people started to talk among themselves. "If that was my boy, I would have told Mr. Macker no. I would not whip him."

It was the first time anyone had ever heard the one-eye man speak out. He stood up and looked across at the other people and said, "If this had been your boy, you would have done the same thing. You would have whipped him just as I did because you was told by the white man to do so. If you are so damn smart, then why are you out here picking his cotton? Whether any of you know, I am educated; I can read, I can spell, I can do math, but what good does it do me? I am still just a nigger. Being educated caused me to lose my eye. I know all of you call me the one-eye man. My name is Ben Nolen and Philip is my grandson."

Everybody started back to work and Ben then started to tell his story. "I was a slave on a plantation. The master was a fair man. He had a son; his name was Bob. He was a good boy. He always called me Ben, never out of my name. Bob would leave for the field. After all the afternoon chores were done, Bob and me would go out to the edge of the field and he would teach me what he had learned that day in school. I don't think he understood how forbidden I felt it was to teach a nigger how to read, but he continued to do this year after year."

"Over the time, I had grown into a teenager by now. I perhaps could out-read my master. Then one night, some slave grabbers kidnapped me and two more boys from the plantation. We must have traveled for days, then they sold us to another plantation owner. After time went on, I had settled in and started a family. I got careless and started to teach a few children how to read. The master found out that I could read by his top nigger. I was tied to a tree by his top nigger, then he was ordered to start a fire and heat a poker iron until it was red hot while my family and the other workers looked on. My head was pushed back and that red hot poker iron was jabbed into my eye. I was then sold again. That is how I ended up here on the Macker Plantation."

"Once upon a time, I was so determined to learn. I dreamed of sitting in a classroom being taught by a real teacher. I often thought of going to college and becoming a teacher; there's just so much joy in learning – take every opportunity offered to you. It's just a shame what a man will do to another to cause pain to their body and mind, or is there much of a separation between the two? My eye was burned out – body pain. It was done by a black man – the master top nigger. When he was done, he was saying to me, "Niggers don't supposed to read. White people read. Niggers don't." Then he said to his master, "This nigger won't read no more, master. I will see to that for you."

6. txt

The families were disgusted with their shattered dreams and broken hearts. Weak people always come out as the victim. Early the next morning, we were given assignments in order to work from sunup to sundown.

I grew into a young woman, fifteen years old. I had taken a liking to a young man that had come over on the wagon train with us: Mark Waters. He was also fifteen years old. He was going to ask my papa if he could marry me when we turned sixteen.

An older man used to stare at me and talk to my papa. Often, when I would look up at him, he would look away. He was a big man, real big. I had heard when he was younger he was used as a buck. That was the name that they gave a man when they were used to mate with women to have big, strong babies. He had his own little farm at the edge of the Macket Plantation.

Two days before my sixteenth birthday, we were having supper. Papa was quiet, not talking at all. Then about halfway through supper, Papa said to me, "Moellen, Mr. Bud has asked me if he could have you for his wife."

Everybody looked at me, then I said, "Papa, I know you said no, I know you said no, papa."

"Moellen, you are a young woman. Your mama and me has raised you up to be a strong young woman. Mama would never say no to papa."

7. txt

Then he said, "He offered me a prime sire piglet which can be ready to produce piglets next spring, and a rooster and a hen. He will deliver it tomorrow morning and you be ready to go with him."

I heard the wagon coming. My heart was pounding at an enormous pace. He delivered the piglet and chicken to my papa. My papa yelled out, "Moellen, come on out."

I was yelling, "No! no! no!" but to no advantage. I was put into the back of the wagon and he pulled off. I said in a deep voice, "Yes, I do know your name. Your name is Moellen."

The first month Bud was very kind to me, but also very jealous. Night after night, he would take me in his arms and have his way with me. I resented him touching me, but I did not resist him. I would close my eyes and think of Mark Waters. I did it every time. He was so jealous that it led to beating me.

Months passed. I became pregnant with a child. In my ninth month, a young man came by on a horse and asked me if he could have a cool drink of water from the well.

I obliged him with a drink. Bud saw horse tracks at the well, and, without knowing facts, he beat me until I went into labor. A short time later, my son was delivered.

He was given the name Archie.

8. txt

With my battered body, I held my son in my arms while he stood there and looked down at me and said, "Our beautiful son. I want to thank you for having him for me."

After a twelve-hour shift in the field, a woman name Clara, all that day had been saying that she had some beautiful fabric to have her a dress made and how good she was going to look in her new dress. She had a teenage boy named Arthur. He was told by his mother to deliver the fabric to an old lady that made dresses. The old lady lived miles away. Arthur asked some of the other boys to walk with him. They all refused. It was late summer, so there was enough time to get there and back before dark.

About halfway on the journey, there was a couple enjoying a late-afternoon horseback ride coming my way. I jumped from the trail and hid behind some bushes just in case they might decide to pick with me. They went past without seeing me. They went around and came back under the hill down below me. Then they stopped the horse, then dismounted, acting like two typical teenagers in love – running and playing with each other. They stopped and held each other's bodies close together, facing together and slowly started kissing until they both ended up on the ground. Kissing and hugging went on for a while.

Then the boy wanted to go further then just kissing. The girl rejected him. He continued to pursue the issue, but she continued to reject to the point where he became angry. He put his finger in her face, then slapped her, then got on his horse and reached down and got the reins of her horse.

9. txt

He started to leave her out there without a horse. Just a short way away he stopped and returned, dismounted his horse, staring fiercely at her with his finger pointing, yelling loudly. Viciously, then he shoved her, quickly followed up with a second shove.

She fell to the ground. She quickly got up and started to walk away. He caught up to her and grabbed her by the shoulder, spun her around to face him, slapped and then shoved her. She seemed to have gotten her feet tangled on an object falling to the ground. She didn't attempt to get up; she continued to lay there, limp.

He then kneeled down to her, giving her a gentle push with his fingertips while calling her name. Then he put his hand under her head, then quickly pulled it out from under her. His hand was covered with blood. Fear and panic started to take over. Undecided what to do, he looked as if he wanted to set it up as if she had fallen from her horse.

It was time for me to move on. With just a crumble of noise, he looked up and saw me, then he mounted his horse and started chasing me. I ran at the top of my speed but he continued his chase until he was just yards behind. I then turned into the forest, dropping the fabric from under my arm. He was unable to continue his chase because of hanging tree branches.

10. txt

He yelled to me, "I saw your face. I know who you are. If you say a word about what you saw to anyone, I will come after you. I will get your whole family."

Arthur returned home in a frantic stage, keeping silent about what he had seen, remembering the words that had been used by the man, "I know who you are. I saw your face. I will get you if you tell anyone about this." Unknown to his mother, he never delivered the fabric.

Later into the night, several riders rode up to the Lascos' home, Danny's family, yelling out, "John! John Lasco!"

John opened the door just a crack and answered through it, "Who is out there?"

"John, it's Ben Rival."

"Ben, what are you doing here this time of night?"

"Well, John, my daughter Cary is missing. She went out this afternoon and never returned."

"I am sorry to hear that, Ben."

"Well, John, I know she was sweet on your boy, Danny. I just want to know if he saw her or heard anything."

"I will ask my boy, Danny."

John asked Danny if he had seen Cary. Danny answered no, but Danny's whole body was shaking. His voice was scrambled. John knew that Danny had been involved in whatever had happened. Then he returned to the door and denied that Danny had any information.

After the rider rode off, John returned to Danny's room. John used a soft-spoken, but high-pitched voice. Danny then confessed to his pa.

Untitled

"Pa, it was an accident I didn't mean to hurt her."

"Boy, you fool! what happened? Tell me the truth."

"Pa, we were in love and she rejected me. I lost control. I pushed her around a bit, she fell and hit her head on some object. It was an accident, Pa, I swear."

"Where is she now? Is she dead?"

"I don't know, I just left her up there. I was scared, Pa. I didn't know what to do."

"Did anybody see you go up there?"

"Just a colored boy."

"Did he recognize who you were?"

"I don't think so, but as he was running I told him that I knew who he was and I would get him if he told what he saw. He dropped this as he was running away."

"We have to go up there, bring that fabric. Danny, you have become some kind of monster. Do you know what this will do to the Lucas name? Danny, you have more at the age of nineteen than most boys will have in a lifetime."

"John, where are you and Danny going? It's late."

"It's ok, Anne. Go back to bed. Danny and me going for a little ride."

"John, I heard everything."

"I will take care of it, Anne. Don't I always take care of everything?"

Two days had passed. The word had spread across the plantation that a teenage white girl had been found dead. She had been wrapped in some new fabric down in the valley near the trail that Arthur had been taking. Arthur was soon tracked down. He had no chance in the eyes of most people. He was guilty even though he was allowed to tell what he had seen .

But there was no doubt to the law that he was guilty, and sentenced to death.

Midmorning, Ann Mckayle went out for a carriage ride. It was her intention to pass Arthur's parents' house. Slowly she passed as the family took a break from the fields for a lunch break. They sat on the porch eating lunch. Mrs. Mckayle stopped her carriage as if there was a problem with it.

It was unknown to Arthur's parents who she were or why a white woman was out this way. From birth all they knew was to show respect to white people. Arthur's mother was in tears explaining to a strange white woman about her son. The story is sad and heart-breaking. Yet two mothers sat there on the front porch. One of their sons was going to be put to death for the same crime that the other mother's son had done.

"I am sorry, ma'am, but I don't see a thing wrong with your carriage."

"John, we can't let that woman's son die for something our son did. Those people are not animals. They have feelings. They get sad and cry just as we do."

John stared her directly in her eyes and said, "I love you, Ann, but I also love my son. In a few days this will be all over and things will be back to normal."

"Maybe for us, John, but for that poor family, things will never be normal again."

It's been fifteen years, and I had only seen my mama twice since my papa traded me for a pig and two chickens. I now have six children. Archie is a young man. He was a tough cowboy on the plantation: could rope and throw any cow to the ground and have it branded in just minutes.

There wasn't a horse in the county he couldn't break and ride. He would travel around the county with the boss to break horses. He was muscular, handsome, and popular. If you didn't have to work in the fields you would be more popular that the field hands. Archie had more advantages than the other young men on the plantation. Sometimes the boss would let him use the carriage to take his girlfriend for a carriage ride. Then I became a grandmother all over the area. Then he settled down with a woman named Mary. He already had two children by her. My oldest grandchild was a girl named Nancy. She was ten years old before I ever met her.

By the time I was sixteen there were times that my father would take me to the general store with him to pick up items for the boss. It was great just to get away and see some other people. We were on the wagon near the general store and a young man was walking and we stopped to give him a ride. My father asked, "Where are you going, young man?"

"Nowhere special. I am just wandering about, looking for work."

"My name is Archie and this is my daughter Nancy."

"Good to meet you folks. My name is Jim." Jim went back to the plantation with us, and was given some chores to do. He was allowed to live in the barn's attic. I knew that I should get my bid in on him before the other field-hand girls ever saw him. My daddy invited him to dinner.

"Jim, it seems as if my daughter wanted me to invite you to dinner." He asked him in front of me. I was so embarrassed, but he accepted the invitation.

In today's society, Jim could have been an All-American athlete. Sunday-afternoon baseball games, he was the star – diving, catching balls, and he could hit a ball so far. Seems he would get a hit every time at bat.

I remember the first time we kissed. We were sitting on the front porch in a swing. Jim was pointing out the Big Dipper stars out to me. I was laughing and pretending not to see it. He put his right arm around my shoulder, and then put his cheek against mine and pointed with his left hand. My heart was pounding like a bass drum. Then he started to stare at me, then it was on. After two years of dating, Jim and I were married.

September 23, 1982, 6 o'clock a.m. I was awakened by the sound of my alarm clock, just as I had been every morning for the past nine years. I was going to drive into the city to see a doctor. His name was Dr. Sunclay, a psychiatrist. No, I was not crazy – at least I don't think I was, just confused. Fifty dollars for a half hour, I must have been crazy!

I was off to an early start, trying to get ahead of rush hour. Traffic seemed as if everyone had the same idea in mind. I was caught in the middle of a traffic jam and couldn't move. At last I was there, with a brief moment to window-shop before my appointment was scheduled to begin.

I arrived at Dr. Sunclay's office at 9 o'clock a.m. The moment I walked into the office a chill briefly came over me. Dr. Sunclay was expecting me, so we wasted no time at all with formalities. After making sure that I was as comfortable as possible, Dr. Sunclay sat down just across from me.

Then he began talking to me in a deep, resounding voice, putting me deeper and deeper into a hypnotic state. His voice was coming to me as if it were in slow motion. "Mr. Woods," he was saying. "Just relax and let your inner mind become your present. Go back, go back into your past and relive your life. Go back, go back."

"The report I have read on this man indicates that he has an I.Q., as well as the ability, to be President. Instead, he is living in the shadow of his past. We must turn your future into a reality. If a person can control your mind, they can control your body."

"I am going to take you back through the days, hours, and minutes. Mr. Woods, how old are you?"

"Five, I am five years old. I know this because I am too young to work in the fields. My parents would leave me at the end of one of the long roads in the cotton field. One bright sunny day I am laying in a cotton cradle, flat on my back, staring at the beautiful blue sky. A vulture is flying overhead, beneath the beauty of the sky. It seems so free up there, the way it spread its wings and was able to stay up without flopping. You better go away, vulture, Mr. Macker will put you to work."

"As soon as I called him by name, Mr. Macker drove up. I had large eyes – he called me catfish eyes. 'Catfish eyes, run across there and tell the hands that it is lunchtime. By the way, catfish eyes, how old are you?'"

"Five, Mr. Macker."

"Ok, I have to talk with Jim. It's about time you started doing some work around here."

Mr. Tom Macker, plantation owner, very rich, and very powerful in this county.

would a black person."

"Bud, you and Henry will fight tonight."

"Tom won't lose tonight, so I will give you boys the rest of the day off. So you get down to the creek and cool yourselves off."

"This water feels good."

"I need this relaxation."

Henry just picked up a handful of rocks. He did not get in the water. He just sat on a log at the edge of the water tossing one rock at a time into the water.

"Henry, come on in."

"I don't think I want to."

"I don't know just why we are doing this."

"Doing what, Henry?"

"We go down there and fight for Mr. Macker – lots of money for him, and what do we get?"

"Why don't we just leave here? Why don't we just run away from this place?"

He owns everything in sight! Seems like he owns half of the county, in fact, including the people, to

25

some degree. The Macker Plantation is a place where sometimes you wish it would stay night forever. My family and me just happen to live here. My mother Nancy keeps house for the Mackers'. Frances my oldest sister, Alice my second-oldest sister, Bud my oldest brother, Rod, Hank, Jank, and me, Little Woods. Night after night I would sleep jammed between Hank and Jank, barely able to move.

Some nights I would lay awake for hours wondering how it was possible that Mr. Macker has so much when we have nothing. Over a hundred people work on Mr. Macker's plantation. He own hundreds of heads of cattle, thousands of acres of cotton. Pecans, catfish ponds, a moonshine still, the general store, and the old plantation gambling house.

On Saturday night the plantation owners would gather together in the gambling house for all types of gambling. One such gambling included boxing matches. For miles around other plantation owners would bring in their big, tough field-hand boys to participate in boxing matches.

My brother, Bud, is a boxer. He was top boxer for the Macker Plantation. Mr. Macker has two other boxers, but Bud is the best, by far. He is Mr. Macker's favorite. Bud has to fight every other Saturday night. For the past year he held the record of twenty-three and 0. This was his night to fight. On the day of the fight, Mr. Macker would give his fighter the day off from the fields for a brief workout and some rest.

Bob Greenleaf, Mr. Macker's foreman, was the trainer for the fighters, but the way he trained made me feel as if he were the meanest person in the world. He would look at a dog with more respect than he…

"Stop talking foolish, Henry. Where will we go? We don't have any money. We barely know any people besides the ones on this plantation."

"I know how to get money, and lots of it."

"What are you talking about, Henry?"

"Bud, Butch, we can do this."

"Every Saturday night Mr. Macker takes all of the money home from the old plantation house."

"We could just be outside of his house when he get out of his truck, and we jump him and take the money."

"Are you crazy?! Do you know what would happen to us if we do that?"

"After we get off of the plantation, we will be free. We are not slaves. Mr. Macker don't own us. He can't track us down and bring us back."

"Henry, you just get that crazy idea out of your head. If you steal that money the law will be after you. What about Betty Jean? You love her. You said you were going to marry her."

"Yes, I do love Betty Jean. What if we get married and have children here on the Macker Plantation? They will just be dumb field-hands just like the three of us. None of us can read or write. We wouldn't know our name if it was hanging off that tree. I want my children to be educated. Bud, you are good enough to be a professional fighter, but you continue to get your brains beat out and get nothing for it."

"It is time to go. Bob Greenleaf will be coming soon." Late afternoon, the cigar-smoking men gathered at the old plantation house, sat in a smoke-filled room, sipping on their favorite beverages, enjoying their Saturday-night outing, preparing to enjoy a human cock-fight.

Sometimes late into the night, after a fight, Bob Greenleaf would bring Bud home, badly beaten. For the past hour he had been involved in that human cock-fight. Mama would sit by his bedside trying to comfort him.

Later into the night, Big Jim came rushing home with lots of blood on his clothing. Loudly, he was saying, "Nancy Leory killed Charles!"

"Oh no. What happened?"

"I don't know. They were just standing there talking. Then they started to argue loudly. Leory pulled a knife, stabbed Charles three times in the stomach. Charles fell towards me and I held onto him, as his limp body started to fall to the floor. I tried to help, but it was too late. Charles was dead!"

"Did someone tell his wife, Bea?"

"Yes, she knows."

"Did the sheriff come?"

"No, Mr. Macker won't let no law get involved in this matter. The law won't come on Mr. Macker's plantation unless he say so, and he will not say so in this case because, instead of losing one field-hand, he would lose two. He will move Leory and his family to the other side of the plantation until tensions calm down."

That was the first person I have ever known to die, and my first encounter with black-on-black violence. I had nightmares about this for months. I wondered, how could a person intentionally use a knife and pierce the body of another person, causing serious enough injury to cause their death? Big Jim would go along with the boxing beatings. He was angry, along with the other fathers living on the plantation. There was nothing they could do. It was Mr. Macker's decision. After having a comfortable Sunday, late into the night I would lie awake staring into the darkness, with very little hope for a better life.

Sometimes it was as if I could see through a magic mirror that life wasn't meant to be this way. As daybreak slowly arrived, mama would get up and start breakfast. Soon I could hear the coffee pot perking. The smell of coffee and sliced ham, simmering in red-eye gravy, would fill the house with a familiar-smelling aroma. Then mama would call to us, "It's time to get up." It seems like, as soon as she finished making breakfast for us, she had to leave and go over to the Mackers' and prepare their breakfast.

Just halfway through our breakfast, Mr. Macker drove up to our house and stepped out of his new truck. "Jim, I have to give it to you and Nancy – that boy of yours is a born thoroughbred. He went up against a boy almost twice his size and whipped him good. You know, Jim, I already have plans for that next boy of yours. If he do as well as your boy Bud, shoot, I could get me a new truck every month! That is too bad about Charles; he was a good, hard-working field-hand, a true family man. What happened up there, Jim? I gave ol' Tom two gallons of my finest shine to celebrate that new baby boy of his. I thought you boys could get together and have a good time without killing up each other. I

29

would do the same thing for any man and woman on the plantation when they have a new child. Remember, Jim, when that baby boy of yours was born I gave you permission to go over to one of my catfish ponds and catch all the fresh catfish you wanted. I think that is what happened: you had so much catfish around that boy started to look like one. That boy is now five years old. I would have figured that you and Nancy would have had at least two more by now."

"Jim, you go work with Bob Smith in the bottom land today. I will go pick him up and be back in five minutes."

Working in the fields was limited for the girls. They would get a chance to start school. Every morning Frances and Alice would get up early, get dressed in their can-can skirts and white Barbie socks. They would join up with the other girls from different areas of the plantation for a three-mile walk down a dusty rock road to a small one-room schoolhouse. I can picture them now walking home from school. The boys in the field hollering courting words at them. The oldest teenage boys' hormones were starting to act up.

"Doug, you and Frances have been dating for over a year, and all you have ever gotten was a kiss."

"What do you know? You have never kissed a girl before."

"Frances and me will do what we have to do when the time come. I am going to talk to her now."

The other three teenage boys gathered to a huddle. "Fellas, I am eighteen years old and I have never been with a girl."

"Have you, Joe?"

"No."

"Ben, have you?"

"No."

"We don't have to continue to be virgins. I know how we can get a girl. May, she plays down by the barn everyday – we can take her."

"She is a retard. You want to rape a retarded girl? You are crazy!"

"She may be a retard, but she still is a woman, and she can't tell who did it."

Living on the Macker Plantation is just a step above slavery. Once a month Mr. Macker would allow each family on the plantation to make an eight-dollar purchase at his general store for their necessary items. Most of our food was grown vegetables. Big Jim made his trip to the general store.

After more than an hour's walk to the general store there was a few minutes of rest. Shortly after, Big Jim picked out some items: sugar, salt, coffee, flour, and some rice. Mr. Macker, the brother of Mr. Lawrence Macker, ran the general store.

"Mr. Tod, my son stepped on a nail. His foot is infected. If it's possible, could I get some type of medication for the infection?"

"Jim, your purchases have gone over your limit. If you need some medication, you have to put something back."

"Ok, Mr. Tod. Take off the flour and rice." Big Jim gathered the items and started the journey home. "Nancy, we have to leave this plantation. I don't know when or how, but it will happen. We have to keep this idea just between us. Things have a way to get back to Mr. Macker. If this does, he will be watching us closely."

Frances's boyfriend, Doug, came by to see her. "Frances would you like to go for a walk?"

"I don't know. Mama and Big Jim is not here. They went to the general store, and have been gone for a long time. They will be back soon."

"Doug, we have been walking for a while; where are we going?"

"Just going to walk down to the bottom land to enjoy the beauty of nature and talk about the nature between a man and a woman. Frances, you have been my girl for a long time, over a year. We have only hugged and kissed. I love you, Frances.

"I love you, too, Doug."

"Frances, can we experience nature between man and a woman?"

"But Doug, I could get pregnant. If I do, will you stick by me?"

"Yes, baby, you know I will. Then our folks would just have to let us get married."

"I want to, but someone might see us out here."

"There is a cotton barn over there. We will be in private. It is going to be beautiful, you will see. Trust me."

Big Jim and Mama had started a plan to leave the Macker Plantation. Cash money was badly needed. You see, Mr. Macker did not pay with United States dollars. He paid with chips he had made for his people on the Macker Plantation. He called them Macko-chips, and you could only use them at the general store. For weeks, Mama would gather eggs until she had enough for a sale. This would bring a small profit. Then Rod, Hank, Jank, and me would set out for a five-mile walk the back way into town, all the while ducking and dodging Mr. Macker, Bob Greenleaf, and other people on the plantation who would be more than happy to tell him that we were up to something.

Sometimes it would be a hundred degrees in the shade, but we had to continue the journey: failure was not an option. We had to walk through tall weeds, jump over small ditches, and through barbed-wire fences, but we made it to town. With no special place to sell the eggs, we stopped in front of a food store, but not for long. The store owner soon came out and ran us off with some unpleasant words.

Rod told Jank and me to go in one direction, and him and Hank would go in the opposite. Jank and me started walking through the neighborhood, stopping at houses with no luck selling the eggs.

With a lot of humiliation by the neighborhood people, we decided to walk at least one more block. Jank and me started walking for a while.

We stopped in front of a house; choosing it at random, we walked up on the front porch and knocked on the door. After knocking several times, a middle-aged woman answered the door, not friendly at all. Holding a flyswatter, she answered through the screen door. "What you boys want?"

Jank immediately went into his sales pitch. "Ma'am, we have fresh eggs. You can bake fresh cakes and the most delicious pies that anyone could sink their teeth into. They are only 15 cents a dozen."

"You boys get away from my door. Do you hear me? I said you get away from here right now! I mean it. You colored boys don't even have the decency to go around to the back door like all the other colored. Get away from here and don't ever come back!"

She came out onto the porch and shooed us away. As I was jumping from the porch an egg fell from my bucket, not breaking on the soft grass. She picked it up and started to throw it, but decided not to. Jank and me ran a block before stopping. I knew that we needed to sell these eggs – the family depended on us. Although this was my first time experiencing life outside the plantation, so far the experience was less than I expected. Unfriendly people that would say anything to you just to hurt your feelings. Jank and me had been called names, but at the time we didn't know it was supposed to be humiliating. The names we were called, I thought that's what we were.

We went back downtown to meet up with Rod and Hank just to find out that they had no luck, either. By then I was so thirsty I could drink my own sweat.

The only place I could get a drink of water was the fountain across the street, with a sign I later learned, said, "WHITES ONLY," but I couldn't read, so I started to run across the street when Rod grabbed me. He couldn't read, either, but he had heard bad things about colored people trying to drink from that fountain. I asked him, "Why can't I drink from that fountain?"

"Because it is for white people only. White people once lynched a black person for drinking from that fountain. You just going to have to wait 'til we get home."

After a long walk barefoot, our feet were scorched and in so much pain. We ran across and stood in the water from the fountain run-off to soothe our aching feet.

About that time a white man was standing by, heard most of our conversation, stopped and said, "How are you boys doing?"

"Ok," we said.

"Those sure are some fine-looking eggs you got there. How much are they?"

"15 cent a dozen, sir."

"How many dozen do you have?"

"We got six dozen, sir."

"That is just the amount I was looking for." That man took us to his house, gave us some water and bought all the eggs, then told us to bring him some more sometime.

It was about dusk when we returned home. Once again darkness cast a shadow over the plantation. Many ways, sadness comes before the sunrise. I have experienced life outside of the plantation. Unfriendly people encourage me that maybe here on the plantation is where I belong. I made no attempt to explain that I was confused because of the way of the world. I continued to struggle with my emotional disturbances. How should a child have the ability to understand that he should do all within his power to hold his pain?

Big Jim and Mama went on with their plans, even if it meant not saying a word to my brother Jank. I had a seat by the window where I could sit and stare up at the stars. Big Jim was going out to drink with the men – Mr. Macker had set it out once again. Someone had just had a new baby boy. Mr. Macker knew what kept the field hands happy – fill them up with whisky on Saturday night, then treat them like a slave come Monday morning. Bud was off to defend his title.

Now something would happen that I really like. Mrs. Tibbs, an old lady that lives over the hill behind us, had no family and would come over to visit with us. She could tell some of the best stories, but the one that always captured my attention was the true story of the history of the Macker Plantation. We would settle down around the kerosene lamp. I heard her talking, but I continued to focus on the brightest star that seemed to be there just for me, then she would start her story-telling.

She talked very slowly and softly. She would start off by saying, "I tell you this plantation has been in the Macker family for generations and has a very mysterious history. The things that I have witnessed here could only make you wonder why. Oh, I was just a little girl, about five years old, but I remember it like it was yesterday. Now Mr. Macker's grandfather, Lawrence Macker, was a fair man. If you would get into trouble he would know how to punish you fierce, fully. He was the leader of the mob gang. Everybody knew it. This gang was so fierceful terrifying they would go out late at night and terrify black families."

A cross-burning was the most frightening thing that a colored person could experience. I experienced it once as a young girl – even to this day I have nightmares about it. There was this old lady, Sister Harver. Everyone called her that here on the plantation. Her husband was lynched for cursing at a white man, leaving behind a widow and three children: two boys and a girl. There were rumors that Mr. Lawrence Macker would go visit her sometimes, late nights. Tommy Lee was her oldest boy, the blacksmith of the plantation, real good with horses. Once a year, the misses of the plantation would take a trip down to New Orleans to visit her sister. Well, it's about that time of the year, so Tommy Lee had to drive her down to the train station. Tommy Lee was a friendly person, smiled and talked a lot. A great comedian of his days.

"Tommy Lee, move that team along. Don't you have me to miss my train, talking all of your blabber, and go around some of these bumps."

"Yes'em," Tommy Lee said. Tommy Lee was laughing to himself, to see her bounce around as he drove over the bumps. After listening to the misses complain for miles, they arrived at the train station just moments before the train arrived. "See, ma'am, we made it."

"Oh stop your blabbering and get me over there near the station."

Tommy Lee pulled the wagon up to a stop and stepped down. "All these people dressed in their fancy clothing. I wish I could get on that train and just go so far away from here. Someday I could dress just like that, just once, and get on that train and go somewhere. It don't matter where, just go."

Upon hearing the train whistle, a little girl started to get excited. A team of horses, frightened by the train whistle, starting to move around as the train stopped. With excitement, a girl jumped into the air, clapping her hands. The little girl slipped into a puddle of mud.

Tommy Lee stepped knee-deep into the mud to get her.

Just as he was about to step out of the mud, the little girl's mother came. Tommy Lee looked up at the mother and smiled. "She's ok, ma'am," then he winked and passed the child to her mother.

Then she started hollering and beating him on the head with her purse, calling him all sorts of names. About that time, along came the lady's husband and he started hollering at the lady about being irresponsible, and not watching the little girl more closely.

"No, no dear, it was him. It was that nigger. He pushed her trying to catch those horses. We all saw him. He even winked his eye at me. Just ask these people. Go on, just ask them.

"Did anyone see what happened?"

"Just like the lady said, the nigger pushed the little girl, then turned around and winked his eye at her."

"I saw it, too. Yes, that's exactly what happened."

The Macker missus yelled out and said, "They are all lying. The little girl fell." She was told to shut up and get on the train.

There was another black driver from another plantation. No one asked him, but he was shaking his head saying yes, too. He had to think about his own safety.

The little girl's father put his arm out to her, picking her up slowly, turning around and sitting her down out of the way. He turned quickly, backhanding Tommy Lee beside the head, kicking him backwards into the mud. "Get up, boy, come here. Did you push my baby into the mud? I am going to skin your black tail, boy!"

He beat Tommy Lee for a while, then threw him on the back of his wagon and slapped the rear of one horse. As the horses ran away, the man was yelling. "Boy, I am going to get you! You can count on it, nigger."

The horses ran for miles before Tommy Lee managed to struggle up to control and drive the horses home, badly beaten and nearly scared to death. He knew this was not the last time that he would hear from this man.

When Tommy Lee explained what happened to his mother, she called her family inside. It was dark and dreary that Sunday afternoon. Expecting the worst, the dogs from all over the plantation was howling. I tell you it was the strangest thing I ever heard. Days and days passed without anything happening.

One week later, Sunday night, it happened. Just after Sister Harver went to bed, a horsesman rode up to her house and called out, "Hey, hey you, in there."

After a while, Sister Harver looked out her front door. "Yes, sir, what do you want?"

"I am very sorry to bother you, lady, but, you see, I am lost. I been wandering around this valley for hours. I was talking to some of your neighbors, and they said your boy, Tommy Lee, knows this valley like the back of his hand. I sure would appreciate it if he could show me to the main road."

Well, Sister Harver could feel in her heart that something was not right. She also knew she couldn't say no to a white man. The house could be burned and everyone could be killed. She called Tommy Lee. All she could do was pray and hope he returned safe. Tommy Lee walked out and looked up at the white man. He put his hand down to Tommy Lee and pulled him up behind him. Then he turned the horse and rode off over the next hill.

When he turned a sharp curve in the road, there they were waiting, a whole gang of them. Hooded, evil, hateful, white men. When Tommy Lee realized what was going on, it was too late. He jumped from the horse and started to run, but it was too late for that. He was roped and dragged by a horse to a big tree in the area where the gang started their brutal beating. They even castrated him, and then he was lynched to his death.

They dragged his body behind a horse back to Sister Harver's front door, then they threw his badly beaten body up on her front porch with his hands tied behind his back and the rope around his neck.

Sister Harver came out, and when she saw what had happened to Tommy Lee, she started screaming and hollering to the top of her voice. "Oh God, no! Jesus, why? Oh no, oh no, my boy is dead! He was a good boy. Oooh nooo."

Sister Harver and her second son dragged Tommy Lee's body inside and cleaned it up. The next morning Sister Harver had to get up and work the fields like any other day, as if nothing had happened. It was a day of sorrow and mourning in the field. After the day was over, families on the plantation stopped by Sister Harver's to comfort her and help with the burial. They took Tommy Lee's body to the backside of the plantation in a pine box for burial. That was just the way it was.

Sister Harver's second son swore that he would seek revenge on those who were responsible. Sister Harver pleaded with her son, Ben, to just pray and forgive those, and let Jesus seek for revenge."

"Mama I must do this. Our family has been partially destroyed." Ben left that night not knowing what he was going to do or know how he intended to do it.

Ben went into town, waited out back in the dark for a chance to steal a gun from a horse that was hitched in front of a saloon. He was carefully picking his chance. Then it came, and he went for it.

Ben had it half out of the holder when a man came out. "Hey, what do you think you are doing, boy? Hey, somebody get the sheriff. This boy was trying to still a gun off that horse."

"The sheriff is out of town."

"Well, looks like we are going to have to handle this ourselves. Boys, we are going to have some fun tonight."

I was never happier to hear a knock on the door, meaning the end of the story-telling time. Before I realized, it was the end of Sunday morning and on into Sunday afternoon.

Big Jim and Mama were relaxing on the front porch. Us boys were relaxing by the creek, swimming in the cool water. Jank was always clowning around. He said he was going to dive from a tree top into the water, and he did. He didn't realize that the water was that shallow on that end of the creek. His head hit the bottom and stuck in the mud. Some girls, watching us skinny-dip in the water, yelled to us to pull Jank out.

Somehow, word got back to Big Jim and he lined us up to wait our turn. He really put the leather to our backside.

Months later, I was working with Big Jim in the pecan grove. After a week of crawling around on the damp ground, we were only about half through gathering pecans in the grove. About halfway into the morning Bob Greenleaf rode up on his big black horse and walked over to where we were working. He stopped and just stood looking at Big Jim, not saying a word.

After several minutes with an evil look in his eyes, he put his hand in a pail and put several pecans in his hand and started to crack them to eat. He called Big Jim over. "What the hell? You have been working in this grove for over a week."

"Yes, sir, Mr. Bob, but there are over three hundred trees in this grove and they are all just loaded with pecans."

"Jim, I am not here to talk about how loaded these trees are. I am here to talk about what in the hell is taking you so long. If all these groves are not finished in two weeks we could lose 65% of our pecan crop, and we both know that Tom won't like that."

"No, sir, not one little bit."

"So you better get your butt moving and get these pecans gathered. I will especially see to it that you get bounced back into the cotton field so fast you won't believe you ever left."

Big Jim dropped head and went back to gathering pecans. I think he had gotten the message when we weren't allowed to take a water break. For two weeks and one half-day Big Jim worked for fourteen- to fifteen-hour days, even on Saturdays and Sundays. He would leave home before sunrise daily. He didn't stop until all the pecans were gathered and properly stored. This put Bob Greenleaf in good favor with Mr. Macker.

Since Mama worked as a maid over at the Mackers', she would sometimes overhear some important information. Well, Mr. Macker was going to have a brand-new gas heating system and cooking stove. Over the summer, Mr. Macker always had his winter firewood cut. So Mama told Big Jim to go over and ask Mr. Macker for his winter supply of firewood. Instead of Big Jim going directly to Mr. Macker, like Mama had said, he asked Bob Greenleaf to ask Mr. Macker for him.

Bob Greenleaf thought that was a good idea, but instead of asking for the firewood for Big Jim, he asked for himself. He got some of the field-hands to gather the firewood for him. There was loads of wood hauled past our house. Mama was furious, but to keep our plan intact to leave the Macker Plantation, Mama knew we must stick together.

Sunday afternoon, Mrs. Macker wanted Mama to make a special dinner for her guests. Mama had to leave her family without dinner to make dinner for the Mackers. Mama started to prepare dinner for the Mackers. Mrs. Macker was in the kitchen talking to Mama while she prepared the dinner. Then she asked, "Nancy, ain't that girl of yours expecting?"

Mama answered, "Yes, ma'am, she is."

"Lord have mercy, I tell you. How old is she?"

"She is sixteen."

"That would have not happened to a white girl. White girls just have so much more respect for themselves than colored girls."

Mama was angry about the comment, but she put it behind her because, in order for us to get away from this place, we had to keep it together.

Then the Mackers' guests arrived. Mama was serving the guests when Mrs. Macker spoke out and said to their guests, "My maid Nancy's daughter is sixteen years old and she is expecting. I told her how white girls have so much more respect for themselves than a colored girl. Just as those dreadful boys that molested that retarded girl. That was so terrible." Then it remained silent for a while. Then a little girl spoke and said, "Tammy is sixteen and she got expected. I heard you and Daddy say so. You and Daddy sent her to St. Louis to get rid of it."

Mrs. Macker was shocked. She just sat there with her head down, without talking. Then she said, "Nancy, why don't you go out to the well and fetch us some fresh water?"

Mr. and Mrs. Macker was only able to have one child – a son, Bobby Macker. He had been killed recently serving in the U.S. Navy. His widow and young son had arrived today from New York. Mrs. Macker's grandson and I were about the same age. Mr. Macker suggested that I keep him company. His name is Johnny. He is the most spoiled and selfish kid that I have ever seen. I had to go wherever he wanted to go, do whatever he wanted to do. I would follow him around, walking behind him, picking up rocks for him.

Carrying his rock bag, when he wanted to throw one I would get from the bag and pass it to him. Sometimes he would look at me like I was beneath him. Then he asked me, "Why do you always wear those same old dirty clothes with holes in them?"

I answered, "I don't know. Big Jim say I have to wear them."

Then he asked, "Are you a nigger?"

"I don't know. I will ask Big Jim."

"My father used to say a nigger deserves to get just what they are worth, and that is absolutely nothing."

With Christmas approaching, Johnny was always talking about the great gifts he would be getting for Christmas. Since it was only one week until Christmas, nothing could separate me from him. I followed him around as if I were on leash. He never seemed to shut up, but it was ok – the cool places he had been and things he had done, I could only dream about doing. I would picture what the big city was like. Johnny and I were skipping rocks across the catfish pond. I asked Johnny what Santa Claus was going to bring him.

"You are a fool, I don't believe in Santa Claus."

"You don't?"

"No. My father put on a Santa Claus suit last Christmas. I knew who he was when he walked through the door. You have to be a fool to still believe in Santa Claus. My grandfather asked me what I wanted for Christmas. Maybe I will tell him I want a bicycle with a real horn on it. He said if my mother don't take me back to New York, next spring he's going to buy me a pony. That sounds like fun, but I am a city kid, you know. What are you getting for Christmas?"

In my mind I overheard Big Jim bragging about getting five hundred dollars worth of goods at the general store this year. So I was thinking I just might be able to get a bicycle this year, too, and that's what I told Johnny. "I am getting a bicycle," and I also told him it's going to be red with a horn on it.

Just after breakfast a young voice called out, "Woods, come out on the front yard." Johnny was holding a puppy, "Look, Woods. Isn't he pretty? His name is Pucket. Come out and play with me."

"I can't come out because it's cold and wet outside, my shoes have holes in them, and my feet will get wet."

"I have more shoes. If you come to my house, I will let you wear a pair of my shoes – my Mama won't mind. My grandfather dropped me off here and is supposed to pick me up later, but we can walk back to my house."

Johnny had a change of attitude. Where was this burst of niceness coming from? Johnny now carried his own rock bag, and he even gave me one to carry my rocks in. "Woods, I have never had a colored friend before. My father would call colored people, 'them damn niggers.' My Mama would say to him, 'Bobby, why do you call colored people that? It sound so disgusting.'"

"I told her about you last night, that you are my friend. She said that is good." Johnny's Mama, Mrs. Barbara, was friendly to me. She fitted me with a pair of Johnny's shoes, and she even gave me coat.

After hours of playing, Mrs. Barbara called us to come in for lunch. I just stood there wondering if she meant me, too. Then she said, "Come on, little Wood. Aren't you hungry?"

Johnny and me washed our hands and sat at the table. Mrs. Barbara made two plates with a sandwich, potato chips, two cookies, and a glass of Kool-Aid. This was my very first time ever eating store-bought bread. I thought to myself, "Damn, this is good!"

Mrs. Barbara sat at the table across from me. "Woods, we are from New York, the big city. It's sure to have its share of racists. But here, in the South, it is unbearable how unfair a person could be to another person. Johnny has never been around colored people before. He picked up on some nasty habits from his father. I had a talk with him last night. He won't use those words again."

Mama continued to do her work, I knew she had to clean up the mud we tracked in. She did not say a word, but she watched me with the corner of her eyes as I watched her with the corner of mine. "Mr. Macker, it's Christmas. I need more money. This just won't do."

"Sorry, Jim, but understand everything costs more this year. I know I said I was going to give you more this year, but, well, I just can't. Your expenses here at the general store came to eighty-eight dollars for eleven months, and fifteen for the month of December, which is a total of one hundred and three dollars."

Big Jim and Mama looked at each other. Then Big Jim stood up. "Now, Mr. Macker, this here just isn't fair. I crawl on my hands and knees up those pecan groves. Whether it was wet or dry, everyone of those pecan groves were gathered. Our oldest boy goes down to that plantation house and gets himself beaten up whenever you want him to bring you in a profit and entertain you friends."

While Big Jim was talking, Bob Greenleaf walked in. He walked up to the desk and looked at Big Jim, then at Mr. Macker. He said to Mr. Macker, "Tom, you let your field-hands talk to you like this? I think you are more than fair to these people. They don't have to worry about a damn thing. If they do like they are told, they have everything they need."

Mr. Macker said, "Jim, you and Nancy can go on in the general store and make your purchase, and five dollars worth of Macko chips, which you can spend at a later day."

Big Jim balled his fist up so tight you could here his fingers cracking. Then he pounded it on Mr. Macker's desk three times while looking directly at him, and said, "Mr. Macker, me, along with my whole family, have busted our butts for you all year. This is the thanks we get?"

"Jim, this is what you are going to get. If you want it, take it, and get out of my office. Now get! Nancy, you are no longer needed to work in my house. You will go back and work the fields where you belong. You people don't appreciate a damn thing."

Big Jim walked on out the store, and Mama went over to the store counter to wait for her turn. When she was at the counter, Mr. Tod asked her, "What can I do for you?"

The first thing Mama asked for were the necessary things, meaning flour, cloth, thread, and a few other needed items. I looked up at Mama – she looked so sad. Then she looked down at me and rubbed me on the head. She didn't think I realized our situation, but I understand perfectly well.

After we returned home, Mama spent most of the time in the kitchen preparing Christmas dinner, with Big Jim sitting at the table, making plans for our escape from the Macker Plantation.

Before I went to bed I placed a big cardboard box in the corner, expecting it to be filled, but hoping that there was such a person as Santa Claus. "Please, God, let him bring me a bicycle." I laid restless most of the night listening to a cow bell, pretending with Jank that that was Santa Claus.

The following morning I was up early. Before I got dressed I went to my box and just stood looking into it at an apple, orange, and two pieces of candy.

Mama called out to me, but I didn't turn around because I was fighting my tears. Big Jim and Mama told all of us to get on our knees for a moment's prayer. Most of the morning Big Jim and Mama talked secretly about the escape. By now it was mid-day, and I was wondering if Johnny got his bicycle, so I started running all the way from our house to the Mackers' house. Just before I went into the yard Johnny came from around the house on a brand-new red bicycle, tooting his horn. Without saying a word, I just turned around and ran to my favorite hiding place. After a while I returned home for dinner. About halfway through dinner I stood up at the dinner table and said, "I don't want to be black anymore. I wish I was white like Johnny."

Big Jim asked, "Why, son? Why do you want to be white?"

I answered, "Because Johnny gets everything that he wants. For Christmas he got a bicycle, and is going to get a pony this spring, and he don't even have to work in the fields! I don't have anything and probably won't get anything."

Big Jim dropped his fork into his plate and stood up at the table and walked around through the house for several minutes. He called me. We then prepared for a long walk. Big Jim and me walked for miles while he was talking to me about the way it is, and what he was going to do to change it for his family. We settled down to a nice campfire. Big Jim wrapped me in a blanket and placed me on his knee with his arm around my shoulder and said, "Little Wood, you may not understand what I am about to tell you, son, but I want you to understand it as much as you can. You see, son, you don't have to be embarrassed about being black and being called those names. Black people are a very strong and proud race of people, like no other people in the world, with black skin and kinky hair. You see, son, black people came from a far away land called Africa, a land very different from this land. It is a very special place, where time didn't seem to matter, but it was not without its share of problems. There were groups of people called 'tribes.' These tribes were at constant war with each other for many years. Each tribe was involved in a personal war. People fought among themselves. As long as there is more than one person in a single place there will be fights between them. Most people in Africa had never seen a white person before. One day across the ocean came a large, floating object called a ship. It was then that the black man met the white man. The black man does more harm to himself than his enemies does to him."

"They welcomed the white man. Black people are very kind and easy to be taken advantage of. Agreements were made between the white man and the chief of the black tribe to get rid of all prisoners of war forever, and the white man did just that. They brought the black people back to America and sold them for slaves. When there were no more prisoners of war the white man started capturing any strong body – man, woman, or child – in sight. Business was too good to stop now. There were some black people working beside them, capturing black people and turning them over to the white man, perhaps for very little or no profit at all. Breaking up families, taking children from their parents, and parents from their children. Here in America, we were not allowed to learn, not even allowed to worship. We had to honor them as if they were God. Just like today, we work the field all year and only were allowed to get what Mr. Macker allowed us to get. This is how white people took control over us. Even though we are not slaves today, we are still controlled by the white man."

"You see, little Wood, our race has been destroyed and treated so unfairly. In my lifetime I have felt exactly the way you are feeling. You must remember, son, you were born black, and you will die black. There is nothing anyone can do about that."

Months later, Big Jim and Mama had the plans of how they were going to get off the Macker Plantation. It was March, early spring, "We have to leave tonight.

It's either now or never. We can't stay on this plantation any longer."

Big Jim and Mama gathered all of us at the back door with just the clothes we were wearing. One at a time we walked down the back steps. The great escape from the Macker Plantation was about to happen.

It was so dark we could only see a few feet in front of us. Bud and Rod were sent through the front way for a decoy while we snuck through the back fields. We were now on our way, walking at a steady pace. We realized the consequences we would have to face if we were caught. Traveling at that time was probably not a good idea for Frances. She was expecting to deliver her baby in just weeks. If we were caught on the trail chances were somebody would be shot, just to warn others never to attempt to escape the plantation. We stood a good chance not getting caught. After all, who would be expecting us to be out here?

So we traveled on at a normal speed to the best of our ability. It was a struggle for Frances just to keep up, but it was a must that we continue without a break. The journey was hard and was getting harder. We went through corn fields, cotton fields, stepped in mud and cow manure. We were deep into the back fields of the Macker Plantation, miles into our journey.

We spotted a light – it was a hunter's light. Big Jim called out, "Get down, everybody. Get down!"

I was sitting straddling Big Jim's neck across his shoulders. We started moving low to the ground. The light from the hunter came towards us. Big Jim said, "Everybody stop!" The hunter focused his light directly at us and we stared directly back into it. We had no idea who the hunter was, but we were sure that he knew who we were and what we were doing. The hunter turned and walked away. Then we continued our journey with a faster pace. Mama and Alice took Frances under each of her arms to pull her along with more speed. Mama had been writing for months to relatives who lived in the next county to pick us up at a designated point.

Again, Big Jim said to everyone, "Stop and listen." Miles and miles behind the hound dogs were starting to bark. The hunter was on to us and the message had been transferred to Mr. Macker. The message was clear, "You don't leave the Macker Plantation. If you live here, you grow old and die here. Those are the rules, and there are no exceptions to the rules."

We were moving fast because there was still a long way to go. Big Jim, unable to see what object he was coming up on, tripped into a barbed-wire fence, cutting himself badly. There was supposed to be a truck waiting for us at the destination. If it wasn't there we could be in serious trouble. If there was, we just might make it because those hound dogs were getting closer by the minute. The were probably led by Bob Greenleaf, but he would be too late because here was our truck yelling to us, "Here, over here, hurry."

We climbed on back of the pick-up, started to leave. Bud and Rod were not with us, so we gave them a few more minutes. The hound dogs had made it to the truck, attempting to jump on after us. Now we could hear the sound of a horse coming. The truck had to pull off slowly, then it started to pick up speed. Shots were fired from Bob Greenleaf's gun, hitting the side of the truck. Along the way, out jumped Bud and Rod.

"Get on the truck quickly." Everyone was cheering as we drove into the next county. After daylight, we settled into a one-room shack across the field from some relatives. Big Jim needed to see a doctor badly for the cuts he got from the barbed-wire fence. But instead, grandfather wrapped it with pork fat in a white rag to drain out the infection. For several days Big Jim fought off a hundred-degree-plus fever.

On the third day his fever broke, so he was going to be ok. Thank God for his recovery. Grandfather farmed thirty acres as a sharecropper.

It was not farming season yet so we were finally going to get a chance to attend school. My very first day attending school, I didn't know what to expect. At this time we walked out to the main road for a school bus. When that big yellow bus pulled up to a stop, excitement was at a high point. By the time the bus stopped for us, there was so many kids aboard the bus, it was barely possible for us to get on. The bus driver yelled out, "Move on back! All of you just move on back!"

Then he would throttle the bus engine, then he would pop the clutch and everyone just fell backwards. All of that sitting in one spot all day was going to take some getting used to. I was up early for my school day view. My first day of school was just for introduction. After my first week of school I had gotten used to sitting in one spot most of the day, without moving. After all, the teacher was very strict. So far I had seen him make boys taller than him bend over, touch their toes, and he popped them, ten pops on their behind with a perfectly shaped hand-fitted wooden paddle. At first

I didn't know how to write or spell. The school was a two-room house. The first, second, and third grade in one classroom, and fourth, fifth, and sixth in the other room. There was one teacher to a classroom, and about twenty children in each grade. I was most likely not to learn anything. I was never called on during the first month. Every morning we would start out with spelling, and there were hits across your rear end for each word that was misspelled.

So I got twenty hits everyday. After the whipping I had to stand facing the wall for an hour. Jank and I spent all of our recess time together. We were often laughed at and called the "rag boys." "Old, dumb, rag boys, can't even spell their names. That is why the teacher keeps whipping them. They are dumb!" Our shoes were tied with wire to keep the soles from flapping and our clothes had patches all over them. Jank and I felt terrible until we decided to have a talk with Big Jim about it, but it was nothing compared to what he had gone through. Big Jim had heard a news broadcast the week before about some government construction job openings, and they would be hiring about twenty-five labormen. "I walked half across the county, lucky for me my shoes already had holes in the bottom or I would have walked holes in them during the walk. When I walked up to the construction site there were some white men standing near a barrel fire. I went over and asked who was doing the hiring. No one said a word. Then I asked again and they all just laughed."

"Then one of them turned to me and said, 'What do you want, boy? You don't think you are going to get a job around here, now do you, boy? These jobs are for white men only. No one in their right mind is going to hire a damned nigger to do construction work.'"

"I noticed I was the only colored man out there. I said, 'I am not a nigger, and I am not a boy. I am a full-grown man just looking for work to support my family. I can do twice the work of each one of you. Like I said, I am looking for work.'"

"'By the way, they are looking for men with experience. Do you have any experience?'"

"'No, but I am a hard-working man and willing to learn. Now can someone please tell me who is doing the hiring?' Again, no one said a word. I hung around for hours, but no one would give me any information. So here I was without a job. With grandfather passing away just weeks ago."

That night at the dinner table Big Jim told the family that he was going to leave for Louisiana to work on a sugarcane farm. He could earn money to help the family and maybe move us there into a better environment. Two days later Big Jim gathered with some other men from the area to make the trip. I was sad to see him go, but he explained to me that it was the best thing to do for the family.

Things were not the same around here without Big Jim. During the first month we received a letter from him weekly, with some money inside. Big Jim had very little education, so most of his words were misspelled. Mama blundered through his letters. Midway through the second month, we had not heard from Big Jim in two weeks. Mama continued to write everyday, but she never received an answer again. Seemed Big Jim had abandoned us. Mama looked into her purse and there was only thirty-five cents. She did not know whether to send one of us to the store for some neckbones for dinner, or to give it to the neighbor to take her into town for some free food in the commodity line. She decided to give it to the neighbor for a ride into town. Mama stood outside in line for hours in the freezing rain. Finally she made it up to the door. She was asked if this was her appointment date. Mama answered, "No, sir."

"Well, when is your appointment date?"

"Sir, I don't have one."

"Well, lady I can't help you. Next, please."

"But, sir I have no food for my family."

"Lady, there is nothing I can do for you. Please step out of the line. Next."

Some of the kind people in the line made a kind offer to Mama. If she waited she could have some of their food. Some of them passed her grits and oatmeal.

After a meal, those yellow government grits became not so appreciated.

It's now been two years since we heard from Big Jim. We returned home from school. Mama was sitting with her face in the palm of her hand, crying. I walked up to her and said, "Mama, don't cry."

She said, "Jim will never come home again."

"Yes he will, he always come home when I call him. Big Jim, Big Jim, oh please, Big Jim, come home!"

Mama took me in her arms and held me tightly and said, "I am sorry, baby, but your father will never come back again. He is dead. He was killed in an explosion."

Mama wanted badly to go to the funeral. Grandmother borrowed the money for a bus ticket to Louisiana. She arrived at the funeral home just moments before the service started. At the burial, Mama noticed that people were gathering up to this lady, giving her their sympathy and blessings. Mama went over to her and said, "I am sorry, ma'am, you must have been close to Jim, too."

"Yes, ma'am, Jim was my husband and these are our two children, Little Jim and Nancy."

"Tell me, ma'am, how long have you two been married?"

"A year and ten months, and these were the best months of my life. Please, ma'am, you asked if I was close to Jim, too. Are you a relative of Jim?"

"No, I am just a used-up mistake. Excuse me, please."

"It was nice meeting you."

Just weeks later grandmother passed away. We thought that life was unjustified for the human race. Why? What is this? How could this happen to us?

It seems that everything that was going right was now going wrong. We continued to live in a one-room shack. One afternoon we heard Mr. Burfor coming on his big red horse. This horse was the Cadillac of the horses, on that hard clay, mud, wagon-packed road. We could hear that horse trotting from a good ways away. He was coming to see us. "Good evening, Nancy," he said. "Nancy, I am going to get right to the point. The thirty acres that was worked by Jimmy, I am going to let another working family work it, and I will be moving in Jimmy's house, and I will also need this house. I don't think you and your family will be able to work it properly."

"Mr. Burfor, me and my family could work these thirty acres. Please give us a chance to try."

"Nancy, I just don't think you and your family could work it as properly as this family. I am going to need this shack for the family that's going to be taking over this area. A week should be enough time for you to find some place to go."

With no place to go and no idea where to start looking, Mama struggled and was able to find a place on a farm near a railroad track. Rent was ten dollars per month. We were allowed to work the fields to pay the rent. Days after we moved in, the most exciting thing we experienced was watching the train pass. We would guess among ourselves how many cars was on the train and then count them as they passed. We were still at an all-time high struggle just to make it for the family. Sometime, just to earn a little money, we would gather corn from a field that had been harvested to sell some. Some of the corn was used to beat into cornmeal so that Mama could make bread for us to eat.

Our eyes would burn from the smoke-filled house coming up from the busted-up wood-burning stove which Mama continued to prepare a meal on.

It was winter, 1968 I returned home from school along with my two young sisters, seven year old Patricia, and six year old Annie it was a typical day. Mama tried to explain to us why she had very little supper to serve, when you start your day hungry it is difficult to sit in class and comprehend on your studies. But day after day year after year there were times when such situation exists. There were times when my stomach would growl so loudly, causing my classmates to laugh out. The teacher would make me go to the bathroom just to further embarrass me. She knew it was embarrassing because as I was walking out of the classroom, she would also laugh. Then the last bell of the day rang out, and we were dismissed. It would be great but not exciting. There would be so many children on the bus three children to a seat and there were several children standing in front of the ones who were sitting. The aisle would be packed full from the back emergency door, to the front exit door. When the bus stopped to let children off sometimes half the children that were standing would have to get off the bus to make room for others to get off. After nearly a two hour ride the bus is now nearly empty, it is our time to get off. That doesn't excite me because now the journey walking home would take about a half an hour down a mud trail. The mud would sometimes cover your shoes. There would be a small meal waiting for us, but before we could eat we had to do our chores. Gather fire wood for the cooking stove, and then for the heating stove. After we ate we would study the best we could by the kerosene lamp. Then mama read a letter to us that she received from the Mississippi welfare department announcing the food stamp program. But there was still a major problem.

The letter explained that if a person would buy half their food stamps the government would match the other half. Mama's half was forty five dollars, to her that was still a disadvantage. She does not have forty five dollars. After she was unable to purchase her monthly supply of food stamps, weeks into the next month mama was told that a small convenient store owner named Mr. Jim Perry would lend her the money to purchase her food stamps. He would lend her the forty five dollars to purchase her food stamp then she would have to give him back fifty dollars in food stamps. And with the remaining forty she would have to spend it at his store. The store would have very few selections because other people would the same situation to purchase there food stamps. Mama had no other choice but to except this offer, but I thought it was great seems that it had never been so much food in this house at one time. I clearly can say this is the first time I went to bed with a full stomach. Every month for two years Mr. Jim Perry would purchase mama's food stamps. When mama went into Mr. Perry's store for her monthly supply of food she paid him his fifty dollars the store was nearly empty with food supply. This is when she decided to tell him. Mr. Perry I am going into town where the prices are much lower and there is much more choices to choose from. Mr. Perry's wife was at the cash register checking out another customer. Just as mama made her announcement she came rushing over. Jim I don't believe these people, if it wasn't for you they wouldn't be getting any food stamps at all. You do this big favor for them, now they want to take their food stamps and spend them elsewhere. Tell them to just go on get out of here, and don't bother to come back next month.

Time passed and we grew up. Frances and Alice were married, Bud left for Chicago with dreams of becoming a professional boxer, Rod and Hank were farm-hands for the land owner, Jank had lost his right leg in a hunting accident, I was working long, hard hours giving Mama most of my money to help her with her finances, saving a little for myself.

As time passed, my savings grew. I am a young man now, making most of my own decisions, I have been dreaming of the future. Working on a farm was not going to make it for me. Chicago was where I needed to be. I was going to Chicago to live with Bud. Me and Mama made the decision about it. After discussing it, the final decision was yes.

"And good luck to you, son, Mama love you." I was going to leave on Saturday, which was two days from today. I have always dreamed about the big city. Nothing prepared me mentally about what to expect. Saturday morning I was up early preparing for my trip. As the day progressed time was growing closer. Then it was time for me to leave. My adopted grandfather drove me to the train station. He gave me some facts of life but it was nothing I hadn't heard down by the swimming hole back on the Macker Plantation. All of a sudden that big train pulled up and stopped. I slowly climbed on board and had a seat. "All aboard," I heard twice. This is from the city of New Orleans, heading for Chicago, then slowly it started to pull off, picking up speed as it went along.

I tried to sit back and relax. Unfortunately, strange people and places kept me at edge. Finally, I was able to relax. I was listening to the train wheels click from one rail to another. Each time the wheels clicked I knew that we were moving farther and farther away from this place. I just sat back and relaxed with my eyes closed and thought of these reminding thoughts. I was born in Mississippi during a time when life wasn't so pretty, my parents were always there to shelter me with love and affection. I grew up strong. Now I am looking for the right direction, and maybe I will find it in the city. I was surrounded by certain things that weren't so pretty. I had to leave here and take my chances in the city. My father worked those long, hard hours and sometimes didn't make a dime. My mother would go and clean the house for others and would scrub the floors for long, hard hours and get no pity. My sister was tall, black, and pretty, short skirts and long pretty legs. She wore old clothes but they were hardly ever dirty. Bud is a good fighter – he could out-fight many, but how could he continue when not making a penny? When my father went to look for work, he knew his chances were slimmer than a needle in a haystack.

After a twelve-hour ride on a train, it was now pulling into a Chicago terminal. "Man, big city, bright lights." I stepped off the train looking around at people going about their own business. I was scared fiercely. I made my way to a telephone and called the gym where Bud was supposed to be training. The answer I received was that no Bud Woods was training at this gym. I continued to call over and over again and always got the same answer, and it just came to the point where I just got hung up on. What am I going to do now?

Here I am in a city of three million people and the only one I know is Bud, and I can't locate him anywhere. I spent hours walking to and from the washroom until the janitor noticed and asked me if someone was going to pick me up.

"No, sir," I answered. "I am looking for my brother. He is a boxer. Every time I call where he is supposed to be no one has heard of him. I don't know what I am going to do."

"Where are you from, young man?"

"I am from Yazoo County, Mississippi."

"Oh, yeah? That is a nice place to be from, and I do mean a long ways from."

"Have you heard of it?"

"Boy, I picked cotton on a plantation for years. When I got old enough to sneak away I hopped a freight train over thirty years ago without a dime in my pocket. People helped me, total strangers, and gave me a chance and I made the most of it. Now here I am at your service. Can I help you in any way, because you are not going to be able to stay here? People don't give a damn about you here in the big city. They will take advantage of you in a second. I'll tell you what I am going to do. I'll be getting off in an half hour. I will take you to my house so you can get some rest. After that I will help you find your brother. Ok, young man? By the way, my name is Rufus Brown."

"I am Little Woods." To trust a total stranger was crazy, but I had no other choice but to trust him and it was ok with me. Rufus Brown turned out to be a good man who did what he said he would do for me. After I had spent some time at his house, he drove me over to the gym where Bud was supposed to be training. I asked one person after another about Bud, but no one could tell me anything about him.

I went over to talk to a coach because someone had to remember Bud, and if someone did, most likely it would be the coach. After talking about Bud and describing him to the coach, he could not remember Bud. "He was the boxer champion back on the Macker Plantation."

The coach then looked at me and said, "Bud Woods," over and over until he could remember Bud. "If I didn't see that face of yours, I wouldn't have remembered him. But only we didn't call him Bud, we called him 'Hollywood.' I remember why we called him that. He had some of the sweetest moves I have ever seen in boxing. He could have been a rising star. Damn, poor kid."

"What do you mean, 'poor kid.' What happened? Where is he now?"

"I don't know. That kid was battered, it was like he had been kicked constantly by a mule. He had fractured bones that were not properly cared for, and I had no choice but to release him from the gym. I have no idea where he is now. He was living a few blocks from here at the Thunder Bird motel."

Rufus placed his arm around my shoulder and asked me if I had anywhere else to go. I answered, "Yes, I am going over to the Thunder Bird motel and find my brother."

I thanked Mr. Brown for what he had done for me. Then I walked several blocks to the Thunder Bird motel. The moment I walked into the motel I was approached by a glamorous-looking woman.

"Are you looking for a date, sugar?"

"No."

"Well, sugar, are you looking for a girl?"

"No, I am looking for a boy. Bud, my brother."

"Gee, you are looking for a boy." I had no idea why she was offering herself to me. I was totally ignorant to prostitution.

At that time a young woman came down the stairs, crying. A man was following her, yelling, "I have reason to believe that you have been holding out on me."

"No, no, Sugar Love, I will never hold out on you. I promise to bring you every penny I make, I swear."

Then she went into the street. I went out behind her and called to her.

"Yes, what do you want?" When she turned and looked at me her lips were bleeding and her eyes were swollen.

"I know that you are on your way to work, but don't you think you should put on more clothing? Maybe that is why he was hitting you and ordering you to make more money, and bring it to him."

"Don't you understand? I am his woman. I belong to him, and I have to make money for him. My man, Sugar Love, needs lots of money to keep up his sporty image. He has to hit me. He says it's to let me know he loves me."

"Where do you work?"

"I work right here on this street corner. Hey, you have to go. My man, Sugar Love, will be watching me."

I went across the street and sat on a bus stop bench. An elderly woman came and sat beside me, then a young man came and sat beside her. Without talking or anything, we were just sitting there. He grabbed her purse. She tried to hold on even after she fell to the ground. Then he tried to kick her in the face until she let go. Then he started running. I grabbed him from behind, then wrestled him to the ground until the policeman showed up. The woman offered me a reward, but I refused to accept anything.

"Young man, if there is anything I could ever do for you, here is my phone number. Call me anytime, day or night."

Later in the afternoon, I returned back to the motel and settled into a room at the end of the hall. Late that night, I heard a woman begging, pleading, with Sugar Love. "I need a fix so bad my whole body hurt."

"Get the hell out of my face, you ugly slut."

"Sugar Love, please, I need it badly. I will make lots of money for you, I promise."

"You will do that, anyway. Here! You know I was just playing with you. I was going to give it to you. Now get out of here. I don't want to see your ugly face no more tonight."

A short time later there was a knock on my door. "Hi, sugar, I don't think that we have been properly introduced, my name is Jackie."

"Yes, I know. My name is Little Woods."

"Little Woods? Why Little Woods?"

"I don't know. It's just what everyone calls me."

"Well, why don't you drop 'Little,' and just say, 'Woods.' It's good to know you, Woods."

"Well, what's up, Jackie?"

"Nothing, I just want to talk to someone. Somehow I thought you could use a friend, too."

"Thank you for your kindness. I was a bit lonely. Excuse me for asking, Jackie, but what kind of work do you do on a street corner?"

"Woods, I am a prostitute. A whore? A hooker? Ok, you still don't get it, Woods. I sell my body for money."

I looked at her hand and part of her pinky finger on her left hand was missing. I wondered who would buy a finger.

"No, Woods, I sell sex for money – not my body parts."

"No, Jackie, you are too pretty for that."

"Why are you doing this? You could have any man you desire."

"I do, but it's not the man I really love."

"But I heard you tell Sugar Love that you love him."

"Yes, I have to tell him that."

"Why?"

"He owns me and I can't leave him."

"He owns you?"

"Yes, Sugar Love owns me."

"How?"

"Woods, I ran away from home when I was fifteen. I had a little misunderstanding with my parents. I ended up here on the streets of Chicago. No money, no place to go, and no one to turn to. I was scared, very scared and hungry. One day I was just walking and minding my own business, and this big purple Cadillac pulled up beside me and the window rolled down. A big smile came from inside, along with some kind words. No one had smiled at me in months. I immediately got inside his car. He took me to a small diner and fed me. Just the words and a smile seemed to be all I needed. Then we went shopping for clothing. For weeks, I was his show-thing and I was beginning to enjoy it. Then, one night after a good time on the town, he took me back to his room. He sat back in his big lounging chair looking at me, continuing to talk nice, smooth words that he knew I would enjoy. My mind was dedicated to him. I felt that I owed him, and would do anything that he asked me to… so I thought. Then he called me over to him. I will never forget that night. He kissed me so warm and passionate, I had never been kissed like that before in my life. Here I am, a fifteen-year-old girl, and this was a full-grown man. My mind was under control. I fell in love."

"Then he stared me directly in my eyes, holding my cheeks tightly with his fingers, and said, 'baby, I need you to start making some money for me.'"

"I said, 'Sugar Love, I will start looking for a job tomorrow.'"

"'No, baby; no, sweetheart. Jobs won't work for me. I mean I want you to start walking with the other girls.'"

"'No! No, Sugar love! I can't, I thought I was special to you!'"

"'You are, baby. This is why you have to do it! I need you to do it for me.'"

"'No, Sugar Love, I can't, and I won't sell my body, not even for you.'"

"'What did you say? You have the nerve to tell me no, after all I have done for you?' He grabbed my shoulders so tight, with such a powerful grip, I thought he had cut off my blood to my brain. Then he shelled me against the wall, his fingerprints were left in my skin. He grabbed me again, staring me directly in the eyes, gritting his teeth together so tightly I could see the muscles in his jaws standing out. H was saying these words through his teeth, 'Baby, I don't think you understand; I am not asking you to do this, I am telling you. You will walk with the other girls starting tomorrow. Do you understand?'"

The next night I did my first walk. I was so scared. I made no money, and my mistake was trying to run. I had no idea Sugar Love was watching me. I ran and ran for several hours. He soon caught up to me, took me back to his place. The moment we walked through the door he knocked me to the floor. Sugar Love went into his pocket, pulled out a knife. I thought he was going to kill me. I screamed and begged for my life, I thought I was going to die. He balled up my hand inside of his with just my pinky finger sticking out. He cut off my finger. He said, 'this is just a warning. The next time I will cut off an ear.' Then he took me and shot me up full of dope. He could be so warm and charming, Sugar Love could charm the bark off a tree. Then in a split second he would turn cold as ice."

"Excuse me, Woods, please excuse me from my emotions."

"Now on to you, baby. I heard you were looking for your brother."

"Yes, Bud. What do you know about Bud?"

"Maybe I have said too much already. I have to go."

I jumped up and grabbed her by the arm and said, "No, no, Jackie. You have to tell me what happened to Bud."

"Sugar, get your hands off me, I am going to tell you this and that's all I am going to say. He got involved with Sugar Love," she said in a soft, whispering voice. "You better be careful, Sugar Love is bad news. I have to go."

The next day I peeked around corners and through windows at Sugar Love. I was trying to gather enough nerves to approach him about Bud's whereabouts. When I opened my door to peek out, Sugar Love was standing there. "Boy, do you want to ask me something, or tell me something? Why do you keep peeking at me?"

"I want to ask you something about my brother, his name is Bud. He used to live here."

"I know who you are talking about. What do you want to know about him?"

"I want to know where he is or what happened to him."

"Information don't come free, boy. That information is going to cost you."

"I don't have any money."

I didn't ask you for no money, boy. Just make this delivery for me. Take this package to this address. Give it to a person who's called 'Pops' and bring me the package back that he give you. After you return I will tell you where your brother is."

For days I continued to make deliveries with no knowledge of what I was carrying or bringing. After each return, Sugar Love would promise to me just one more delivery and I will take you to your brother.

On the way back from a delivery, I took a break across from Jackie's corner. I put my head down and started crying. A young woman sat beside me and said, "I thought a man was not supposed to cry. Something tells me your tears can't be held inside. Are you ok?"

"I don't know anymore."

"What is your name?"

"My name is Woods."

"Nice to meet you, Woods. I am Rose. I was about to take the bus to Jewtown. You look like you could use a friend, and I could use some company. Good food, good music. If you like the blues then it's the place to be. Would you like to go with me?"

During the walk around I found out that Rose was seventeen years old and a senior in high school. She lived with her aunt in a boarding house and loved the blues. One week ago her aunt had collected her rent money and was on her way to the bank and had an attempted purse-snatching. Her purse had been recovered by a young stranger.

As we walked around Jewtown, blocks away we could here a band playing this song,

You know my baby told me,
And it was not so long ago,
She said I don't love you daddy
And you got to let me go.
You know that was too much for me,
That's why I walked the back street and cry.

Rose jumped out in front of me, several feet, and started dancing to the music. She had a nice dance movement, exciting me.

She put her hands out to me. I said no, because I had never danced in my life. It was so exciting down here, street corner vendors, great food smelling all over the place. After all the daily activities I had been involved in I had gotten totally distracted from delivering this package to Sugar Love. I couldn't deliver it now. I couldn't even go back there.

Charles and Don spoke very highly of you on behalf of becoming a supervisor. We could use a strong leader such as yourself. You could work with the people. See what is their problem? We are a strong working group. We don't need a union with your strong voice in motivating people. People will follow your lead. Your salary will increase tremendously. Money is very important. Charles, you will be able to take your family on that long-awaited vacation. There isn't a person in this building that wouldn't give their right arm to be in your position at this moment. After you accept this position, and I am very sure you will, think about this. Turn yourself upside down, let the loose change fall from your pocket, watch all the unfortunate charge after it. When you then go down, you put your foot on their head and squash their nose into the mud. You're supposed to have no gift toward dogging a person, because if they get the chance they will do the same to you.

I am not sure what to do with this package. Rose's aunt gave me a discount rate in her boarding house, not far from the Thunder Bird motel, so I had to keep a very low profile because Sugar Love would probably kill me now. There was lots of money in the package. Rose and I explored the city and enjoyed spending Sugar Love's money.

After a full day of enjoyment, I realized that I needed a job. With no skill and very little education, finding a job would be difficult. Sometimes I would just stand on a street corner wondering which way to go. There were times I would pass an application. All I could read on it was name and address. I had to keep on searching harder day by day. I knew God would make a way, and God blessed me with a decent job.

Rose and I started to date because she became my best friend. I felt so comfortable when I was with her. After some weeks, I was spotted by Sugar Love; he was not in a good mood. He chased me for blocks but to no advantage. After time went on, I continued to work hard during the day and attended school at night. I studied several classes, including photography. For the first time in my life I felt strength and confidence in myself, and it feels good.

After a year in living in Rose's aunt's boarding house, Rose and I ended our relationship. I purchased a nice house in the suburbs. I had been working hard and had saved most of my money.

I was in my last week of photography class, and my photography instructor had some information for the class. "Listen up, class. Ok? This is your final week, and Friday you will take your final examination. Everything that you have gone over this week and will go over will be on your final examination."

"I strongly recommend that each one of you be on time, because I will not hold class up for anyone. I looked over your past assignments and some of you did ok, some of you were fair, and others need improvement. For instance, if you are photographing a peacock, be patient… it's probably going to open its beautiful tail feathers, and that will make a glamorous highlight. As you did earlier in the semester, I want you to team up with your partner, or you can switch to a new partner. It doesn't matter to me one way or another."

Once again I teamed up with a young lady, her name was Brenda Rodgers. She carried herself as if she was already a professional model. We got together because we were the only two of our nationality in the class. Brenda and I agreed to work at my house on Friday after I got home from work. Brenda arrived at my house a little late.

The moment she walked in the door I noticed that she was impressed. "Nice place. I'm impressed. I am not one to get impressed easily."

"Brenda, would you like something to drink?"

"No, thank you."

"Well, would you like to check out my music collection to see if there is anything suitable for your style?"

"Excuse me, but do you think you can suit my style? I brought my own music.

"Thank you, Brenda, I see that you're the same stubborn brat I teamed up with last semester!"

"You have no knowledge of what it is like to put in a hard day's work. The hardest thing you have ever done was to figure out what outfit you were going to put on the following day! With that attitude, you will never get anything anywhere in this life."

"If you don't change that funky attitude of yours you are going to blow everything that you ever tried to do in life!"

"Well, bless your little country heart."

"Baby, look at me. I am a success. As soon as this simple class is over, I am leaving for New York where my career is going to blossom."

"Brenda, Miss Glamour Girl, just slow down." "Brenda, you don't know a damn thing about modeling out in the real world. The only thing you have going for yourself is your fancy clothes and your pretty face structures, which you are going to fall directly on if you don't get yourself together. You seem to have so much confidence in yourself, and there is nothing wrong with that. Believing in yourself has more power than someone else believing in you. But you are not all that matters in this – we are all in this together!"

"Brenda, I am not interested in working tonight. By the way, my time is valuable, and I don't know when I will be interested in working again."

"Well, fine! I am out of here, Woods. Someone's at you door. You better answer it."

"Hi, baby."

"Rose, what are you doing here? You should have called."

"Oh, you have company!"

"Yes, Rose, this is Brenda. We are working on a class assignment. Brenda, this is Rose. She was my girlfriend for a split second." I made direct eye contact

76

with Brenda. I saw that she was jealous, then she quickly turned her head and walked out.

"So, is that your new girl, Woods?"

"No, Rose, I told you me and Brenda is working on a class assignment."

"No, Woods, I saw the way she looked at you when you made the introduction."

"Ok, Rose, why are you interested in my personal life? Why are you here? What's up with all that luggage? Are you on your way somewhere? It looks like you brought everything that you could fit into the cab." Rose was up to something. I definitely hoped it was not what I was thinking.

"Woods, this is very important. I need a very big favor. Without commitment, is it possible for me to stay here? Just several weeks. I promise you I will be gone in two weeks. My aunt and I had a big disagreement. She put me out! She acts as if I am still a child. I'm a grown woman with a full-time job. I have had it with her."

"Rose, you and I broke off our relationship! That means you go your way and I'll go my way. This will only lead to getting involved with you again, and that will be more than I could handle. I am a very busy person, and I haven't the time for any disturbance!"

"Woods, I promise you, just two weeks and I will be gone! I don't have anywhere else to go right now! Your phone is ringing, Woods."

"I hear my phone, Rose. Brenda, this is a surprise call."

"Woods I was thinking, and you were right. I am just a spoiled brat who is used to getting anything I want. I know what I want! Becoming a professional model won't be easy, my pretty face, sexy ways, and beautiful body won't do it alone. I need your help, Woods!"

"So you think you are beautiful, Brenda?"

"Well, well yes. Don't you? Oh, oh, oh, you don't want to say it in front of your girlfriend! That is it, isn't it, Woods?"

"Brenda, there is more to beauty than just a pretty face and body. You have to know how to carry yourself and have a sweet personality. Treat people the way you want to be treated."

"Woods, I will be over tomorrow night. I am sure things will be better. Will she be there?"

"No, no, Brenda, not tomorrow. I will be busy tomorrow night."

"That's too bad, Woods."

"Bye, Brenda. Rose, your room is to the end of the hall to the left."

"My room, Woods? You are actually going to uphold that? You haven't seen me in six months and you are putting me in my own room?"

"Rose what did you expect? We shouldn't start a relationship that we both know has no future."

"Just kidding, just kidding, I just wanted to see where your head was!"

I almost knew what she was thinking – *Woods thinks that I am just going to walk out in two weeks. I am here to stay! He is too soft and gullible to put me out. I studied his mind, he falls for anything. I'll just tell him week after week that I will be leaving just to keep him thinking I am going to.*

One night later. "Brenda, what are you doing here? I told you I was busy. I am not working tonight."

"Oh, Woods, I just had to get this over with, and I like it here. You have a nice place."

"Thanks Brenda, but that doesn't give you a reason to buzz over at your will."

"Oh, Woods, let's do it. Just look at these modeling clothes. I will put one of these on first."

"Oh, ok, let's do it!"

"Woods, can I talk to you for a moment?"

"Sure, Rose."

"Please, Woods, don't you see what she is up to? She is just a little conniving sneak. She is only interested in you because I am here. She's strutting around here in those skimpy outfits like she's got the hots for any and everything she see that looks like a man, and right now she sees you and you are falling for it! What about that selection of music you are playing?"

"She's a – She's a Super Freak, Love to Love you Baby, Let me make Love to you I won't stop until you ask me to, tell me to, beg me to."

"Woods, that selection is just asking for trouble."

"Rose, what are you trying to say? You and I don't have a relationship anymore. What do you have to do with who I entertain, and what music I play?"

"Woods, why, just tell me why you have a woman here?"

"Rose, if a person is serious about their work, if the music is right, then everything else just falls into place. Goodnight, Rose, sweet dreams."

"Yes, Woods, I am sure yours will be sweet."

Three months passed, and Rose was still living in my house and showing no signs of leaving. During this time I was caught up between Brenda's beauty and glamorous charm, and Rose's innocence, shyness, and delicateness. I don't understand how to deal with two very different people. Maybe I don't understand myself. You see, sometimes I just get so shook up inside and dedication has no meaning. I know what I am thinking, and I also know what I have seen, and the view was not always pleasant. I was insincere and very easily intimidated. Life is such a mystery, love is a crazy game, but I am going to stand tall like a soldier and look into the eyes of my enemies. In emotional times, your heart creates sorrows you can barely bear.

"Woods, what's wrong with you?"

"I don't know, Rose. I am just so frustrated with my life, but I will be just fine."

"Woods do you remember my little cousin Regina that lived in the housing projects? She is now fifteen years old and she is pregnant. She has had the baby, and she is going through some difficulties. She is not doing good at all. I would like to be there for her. Woods, will you drive me to the hospital?"

"Rose, it is one o'clock in the morning and below zero degrees outside!"

"Woods, I need to be there. She needs me. Please be reasonable and take me. Please?"

"Ok, Rose, I will take you."

Rose and I rushed to the hospital. We arrived at the nursery just moments before the baby arrived there. The doctor called the family to the side. "I am sorry, the mother did not make it. We tried to save her, we did all we could do."

"Thank you, doctor." Rose and I spent hours at the nursery window looking at that little infant who was so small and so blind to the world and its giant problems. Tears formed in my eyes and rolled down my cheeks. On a cold and gray Chicago morning another little baby child is born in the ghetto. As it lay there with its tiny little eyes closed, it was not aware of the ups and downs of the ghetto. Its mother died in the ghetto. Its father wanted sex because he knew he could get it in the ghetto and the young mother just wanted to keep her man happy in the ghetto. Its father, a young drug dealer, lots of money, wears *all* the latest outfits and gold chains. All the young girls love him.

"Rose, I remember the first time you introduced me to the housing projects. We took a bus to the area. We were walking from the bus stop to the building. There was little attention to us until we got into the entrance door. At least ten people surrounded us just to ask if we wanted to make a purchase. You said we were just visiting. Then they wanted to know who we were visiting. We continued to the elevator, finding out that it was out of order. Eight flights of stairs. The way Regina smiled when she saw you, although the apartment was disgusting.

Regina introduced us to her stepfather, John. He was having dinner in the kitchen – pork neckbones and cornbread. The introduction did not go well. John barely looked up at us. I continued with conversation. I watched him throw bones across the kitchen at the

81

garbage can. Most of them were hitting the wall and bouncing back to the floor.

In the surrounding area of the housing project, life continued – as the saying says, tomorrow is not promised to anyone. The old people mostly stay inside their apartments. Kids running around, making the most of what they have. There are also some good people that live here, trapped in a world of sorrows. Day after day, life goes on, struggle seems to be a normal life. Some people don't know any better, and some just don't give a damn. Poverty stands out loud and clear.

I look around at people and wonder why? Why us? There are more opportunities for black people than ever before. The word "nigger" rings out so proudly among black people. Women call their men, "my nigga." Friends say to each other, "I love you because you are my nigga." Enemies say to each other, "I will take you out, nigga!" Perfomers make millions of dollars using the word "nigga." Life is like a chain game: one generation follows another in the ghetto. Life is beautiful, but not easy. Some people find out just how tough life is before they ever begin life in the ghetto. There is a time when life seems dark and dreary, so just don't forget to pray in the ghetto.

Time passed, and I felt it was time for Rose to leave my house. Shortly after I returned home from a stressful day's work on a Friday evening, I called Brenda. "Brenda, I am not going to continue to run to your every time. You know how I feel about you. Whenever I try to get intimate with you, you reject me."

"Woods, you know an intimate relationship between you and me would interfere with our work relationship. Woods, I am interested in you, also. There were times when you would walk out of my door to leave, and I grabbed hold of myself to resist from holding you here. Oh, Woods, come over and let's celebrate. I will tell you when you get here."

"Sure, I'll be there in twenty minutes. Yes, Rose, I am going to be there with Brenda so you get off my back. Do me a favor – don't be here when I return. I am not going to let you pull this on me. It's not my style. So long, Rose."

"Woods, no!"

I walked out and slammed the door behind me. I could hear her saying through the door, "I want to have your baby. I want to have your child."

I felt good getting into my beautiful sports car driving off.

"Woods, baby, I am glad you could make it. How was your day?"

"Something is wrong. What's wrong, baby? I can see it in your eyes. Now tell me."

"Brenda, what are we celebrating? You are looking glamorous and smelling terrific. The champagne is sparkling, but not as bright as your eyes. What's the occasion?"

"Woods, play some soft music so we can dance. What I am about to say can change your way of life, the way of our life."

"Oh darn!"

"What, baby?"

"The radio is busted."

"Baby, we don't need music; all we need is each other. Come here and let me hold you. Oh yes, and hold your body close to mine. As the night goes on and the right to be given."

"There'll come a time when we both will go ooh, I can tell by looking at you. You know I played right into your hands. If there's a time we will stop loving, close your eyes, don't think of nothing. Let your thoughts remain inside of your head. May I lay my head down on your pillow? I would like to share the night that's coming on."

"I am tired, but I feel all right."

"I love you, yes I do love you."

"Woods, you have said the right words at the right time. Don't you know I love you, too? I will not reject you now even if I wanted to. You are very special to me."

As I pressed my lips against her perfectly shaped baby-soft lips, every second was treasured into the deepest part of my memory. Early the following morning, I laid holding Brenda in my arms when she said, "Woods, baby, I am glad you are here. What I am about to say can change your life. Let's move to New York."

"I don't know, baby, everything I need is right here, especially you."

"Woods, my agent called yesterday; he has found me work in New York. This doesn't mean the end of us, but the beginning. It's not possible for two badly-in-love people to live and work in two separate cities."

"One week I could fly to Chicago to be with you, and we could make wild crazy love to each other like two mad scientists. The next week you fly to New York again we would make wild crazy love to each other.

"You do have a little wildness in you."

"Every woman has wildness in them. Some of them you just have to bring it out."

"I see I am qualified."

"Baby, you are qualified. You went into new environments. You are hired, the job is yours."

"I knew it was going to rain today. This is so sexy. I love it. Do you like it, Woods?"

"Of course I do."

For days I had trouble facing Rose until she cornered me. "Woods, how long are you going to keep up this little display? You came home after spending the night with your woman. Walked in with the pride of a number-one barnyard cock. Woods, you have a woman living with you, and you just totally disrespected her."

The tears started to roll down Rose's cheeks. I started to feel guilty about my feelings for Brenda. I cared for Rose, but I didn't love her. I wanted her out of my life. Why should I feel so guilty? Maybe I'm just like my mother, too nice. I let Rose live here because I remembered the story about my friend Jackie. With no place to go, and ending up working the streets for a pimp.

"I don't understand you, Woods. Just tell me. You know I am going to be here just for a short time. Could you just be nice and faithful to me until then?"

"Rose, I can't and won't promise you that. I am a busy person. My work is very important to me and I am not giving it up."

"Woods, I am not asking you to give up your work. I am just asking you to have some consideration and feelings for another person. I have feelings, too. I just want to be treated like a person sometimes. I don't think that I belong to anyone. When a person is pushed to the side, that makes them go out of their way for some attention."

"Woods, I have you a nice, hot bath ready. After you have finished with your bath, put on the outfit that's on the shower hanger. I will be up shortly to wash your back. Woods, doesn't that thunder sound lovely? Woods, I am willing to share my love with you on this rainy night. I just want to belong to you. I will be a good girl and I will make you happy. Woods, is there anything wrong with that?"

"No, Rose, there is nothing wrong with caring for someone and wanting to be cared for in return. Rose, I don't have time to prepare for a relationship. I am going for a goal. I want to be like the next Johnson Publishing: I want to create my own magazine company, and that takes lots of time and hard work. It takes obligation and determination. If you don't have a goal to drive for then it will be–"

"I want to belong to you as time slips into the night, raindrops pound against the roof top, lightning flashes across the sky, quickly followed by a burst of thunder."

My feelings towards Rose had changed, having sex had changed.

"When I first met you, Woods, you were sitting on a bench, crying. I wanted to cry, too, and I didn't even know you. I just felt that you were in pain, and had problems. I knew that there was joy behind those tears. Woods, I am just not pretty and sexy enough for you am I?"

"Of course, you are, Rose. You are very beautiful in your own way."

"Well, will you give me some respect during the time I remain here?"

I would not tell Rose that Brenda had left town. I would just say, "Ok, Rose, I will give you all the respect that you deserve."

But what is respect? How deep does Rose want me to go? What is she all about? Two weeks had already turned into nearly a year. Was I here in this big lonely world by myself just to figure it out? Where do I start? Do I start with trust? But trust who? This is where confusion starts.

"Woods, will you come home directly from work tomorrow? I have a surprise for you."

The following day I came directly home, through spring rain showers. I could see Rose waiting at the door. She was wearing a very sexy lingerie outfit.

"What's up, Rose? Do you have company? Candle lights, soft music and dinner?

"No, Woods, this is for you and me."

"Rose, it's raining outside and I am soaked."

"I know it is raining outside, Woods, I planned it this way. I listened to the weather report last night." Rose and I had a pleasurable night.

Months after the mood was gone, I received a phone call at one a.m., unaware that this phone call could change my way of living. When my phone rang a second time, I answered and immediately knew who was on the other end.

"Woods! Hi, baby; it's me, Brenda. I am in town for a few days and I want to see you. I need to see you tonight. Is it possible?"

"No, Brenda, not tonight."

"Oh, Woods, I need you, baby."

"Brenda, perhaps we can meet tomorrow morning. Remember our favorite little coffee shop on Thirty-Eighth Street? We'll meet there at our usual time for breakfast."

I just laid there with my eyes open, staring into the darkness, rolling from side to side, thinking about Brenda, waiting to be with her, touch her, kiss her, and love her.

"Woods?"

"Yes, Rose?"

"You can't sleep?"

"No, I can't."

"Are you going to see her tomorrow morning?"

"Yes."

"Woods, you have to choose between her and me. You are not gong to double-dip the both of us. I love you, Woods, and I can be a good woman to you."

Early the next morning I drove Rose to work. I tried to hold a conversation but there was no response from Rose. She got out of the car and started to walk away. She looked back turned towards me and then turned back and walked into her workplace. I drove off.

I made my way through the early-morning traffic as daylight slowly crept into the sky – the beauty of the morning sun rising over the tree tops and the freshness of the gentle breeze blowing on my face, damp from the fog with someone else heavy on my mind.

I opened the door to our favorite little coffee shop. Yes, the girl was right on time. Loving her was easy; her tender lips were there to greet me. It hadn't always been that way. I could only love one woman at a time. I had to find out where I belong. Every day she makes me do wrong. I opened the door to that little room that she calls home. I didn't feel that I belonged there.

"Woods, baby, is there something on your mind? You barely touched your breakfast, and you are not talking."

This is how I started my day; it's just too bad it won't end this way.

"You don't act very enthusiastic to see me. I am here for you. I want you to come back to New York with me. Everything is working out great for me. You see, Woods, I love you."

"Brenda, living in New York with you sounds great. But, you see, baby, I will not be joining you."

"Woods, why? What is wrong, baby?"

"Brenda, there is only one thing in life I have ever wanted as much as I wanted you. One Christmas when I was very young I wanted a little red bicycle. I didn't get it. My family was too poor to afford it for me. I felt so hurt that, until this day, I have not recovered from that disappointment."

"Can we get on with our future? That was the past, Woods. If you prefer to continue to live here in Chicago, it's ok for now."

"Brenda, I can't see you anymore. I have a bonded dedication with Rose."

"Woods, baby, do you know what you are saying? What has she done to you? This is not you talking. Woods, you taught me so much about myself – without you I don't think I would have made it, and for that I really appreciate you. Woods, is there any chance of you changing your mind?"

"No, Brenda, I feel as if I will never be seeing you ever again."

"I don't believe this. This is not happening to me. I came all the way from New York just to get dumped for her? What is she, Woods? Is she still a nurse's aide? Do you know what they call a nurse's aide? A 'pooper scooper!' You dumped me for a plain Jane? I came all the way from New York just to get dumped? Get out, Woods! Just get out now!"

The moment I walked out that door, Brenda slammed it behind me. I turned and looked back at the door. I felt that I had made a major mistake. As I walked slowly to my car I tried to sing, but the words wouldn't come out. I tried to whistle, but my lips wouldn't pucker. I tried to hum, but a lump was in my throat.

As weeks ended and months came, I continued to ask myself over and over again, "Why, why, why did I reject a woman that I loved so dearly, for a woman that was forcing herself on me." She knows that I don't love her, and I don't think she loves me.

I really didn't want to break it off with her. It seemed as if I had to do it, but for what reason? I don't know. I felt like I was under a spell and had no control of my life. Rose seemed like a good person and she was trying. I was trying to meet her halfway, but most of my time at home was spent in my studio. What's happening with me? Why am I feeling so strange? Sometimes my life seems to be out of control. It's like someone else is controlling me. I don't understand. Rose is now pressuring me to marry her. I am not interested in marrying anyone now. She is a good girl, but I don't want to marry her, but I can't seem to say no to her. I want to, but I can't.

I had to marry her, and I did. Rose had gained momentum, and expected me to be home whenever I was not working. I went along with it. Rose was gaining strength and overpowering my mind. I think back, this whole thing started when I promised to be nice to her just for a while, and she was to leave. Then it started – I was not to speak to any neighbors; when I was driving the car I was to look straight ahead. If a woman was on the curb, she was my woman because I looked at her. Now we would fight because I looked at a woman on the sidewalk.

Knowledge and wit, I was no match, I had no idea what her point or reason was for all of this. After all, she was eight months pregnant. "Don't kid yourself, Woods, pregnant women ain't crazy."

She was pushing me to think that it was me who was crazy. My photographer career was now in jeopardy. My equipment was packed in the back of the closet. How did I get like this? Was I the only man that had been dominated by his woman?

Six weeks later God blessed us with a nine-pound-plus baby daughter. My dreams had not been totally forgotten. To keep hopes and dreams alive I named my daughter Portrait, to keep my mind attached to my dream. After a short time passed Rose was back on my case about everything that I did that didn't please her. I worked the seven a.m. to three thirty p.m. shift. It took me approximately thirty minutes to drive home. If I was five minutes late Rose would be standing at the door waiting for me. I couldn't even come home chewing gum or I would be accused of being in another woman's face.

Rose had me under her thumb, and there was no letting up. Her nails were digging up so deep into my flesh, every time I turned around I felt my flesh squishing through her fingers. I was so sympathetic until I was totally unaware and drained of my self-esteem. Where do I go from here? I am just trying to be a good husband and father. I have to step back and step this thing over. We are all God's children. I have to go away.

"Rose, you and I have to talk."

"Woods, I have no idea of what you possibly want to talk about."

"Rose, have you noticed yourself lately?"

"What is the problem here?"

"Just look around, this house is a mess. Your clothes are scattered all over the place. I could actually plant a vegetable garden on the floor. God knows there is enough dirt on it. I wake up in the middle of the night, several nights in a row, and you're gone. You came in the following morning and stumbled into the house, called your supervisor and lied to her that Portrait, our baby, was sick. How could you do that? That was not the truth. You have become a compulsive liar. You claim for months that there was a hold-up on your check and you were not getting paid."

"I gave you three hundred dollars for bills, and you said, 'Woods, I know you are not going to believe this, I lost the money!' A day later, I gave you a hundred dollars for groceries and you returned home with no groceries, claiming that your purse had been snatched. Rose, one lie that you tell leads directly into another one. Lately it has been one thing after another. I don't believe you anymore. I need to know what's going on."

"Woods, you are imagining things. Furthermore, I don't want to go into this simple conversation. Woods, you are so simple that anyone can tune you up and play you like an old grand piano. Woods, you were crying when I met you and I knew that you were weak."

"Rose, what is wrong with you? Why do you want to play these games?"

"Woods, this is a dog-eat-dog world. Look into my eyes; look very closely." Her voice got deeper as she said, "Woods you are looking into the eyes of the Devil himself, and, by the way, I need a charge; and you know what I am talking about. I have to go get some. Be back later." And she left.

Just after she had left, the phone rang. Without asking any questions, someone said, "Code 666, I received your beep. I have your package, you just make sure that you have my money, plus the money for the last charge yesterday. I don't want no more of your crap from out of your house. I will be at the usual spot in half an hour."

Rose used 666 for her beeper code. 666 is supposedly the mark of Satan. I was still so damn dumb I did not catch on. All I had was my daughter, Portrait. How

93

could a mother just totally ignore her beautiful five-year-old daughter?

Portrait needs a mother and she doesn't have one that serves her any purpose. Where am I? How can I handle this? What can I do? I am just blind, or am I just dumb? No, it can't be that. I just can't find the courage to face her with the real facts. I constantly hurt and have no defense against this new and strange-acting life. It is nearly unbearable for me, as well as for Portrait. I feel as if I've been stripped of my power, and self-esteem is gone. I don't feel I could make a decision without Rose here to make it with me. I now feel like she just went into my body, captured my soul, and locked it away. I am living without a soul, and without a soul I wonder if there is a reason to live.

One afternoon I came home early, and Rose was lying on the couch, burned out and barely able to talk. Several other people were wandering through my house. I yelled to Rose. She slowly turned over and looked up at me, and said in terrible-sounding voice, "Oh, you are home early!"

"Yes, and it's a good thing I am. Where is Portrait?"

"She's in her room."

I rushed back to Portrait's room and she was not there. I called to her several times, but there was no answer. I started to leave the room and then I heard a whine and sniffle coming from the closet. I went over and looked under an old coat; there she was balled up in a little ball deep in the corner of the closet. She was shaking and trembling fiercely. I grabbed her and comforted her with hugs and words of joy. I asked her, "What's wrong? Why were you in the closet?"

"Mommy made me come to my room because she had company. I was so scared, Daddy. I was so scared."

If I put Rose out of my house, she would threaten to take Portrait, and I can't let that happen. If I keep her, what will I do with her when I go to work? I want to put her out and she knows that. She is using Portrait to the fullest. Portrait continued to follow me closely throughout the house. She gave all sorts of information about Rose, her behavior, and activities. When I was not home strange people came over just as soon as I left.

The following day, after I left for work, Rose sat at the kitchen table smoking a cigarette. Her mind was focusing on how she could get her daily supply. Then it hit her: Woods' safe. He always kept money there!

She went to the garage and got a hammer and chisel, and then started destroying the lock on the safe, awakening Portrait from her sleep, Portrait went to her and at that time she was in a frantic stage. She turned to Portrait, dropping the hammer and chisel, grabbed Portrait tight in the collar of her pajamas and pulled her close to her, touching her nose-to-nose, saying, "Do you know what happens to little naughty girls that tell on their moms?"

Tears formed in Portrait's eyes and rolled down her cheeks. Her trembling voice was saying, "Mommy, you are hurting me."

"You shut up. What happens to little naughty girls that tell on their mom? Tell me. Tell me now!"

"They get punished, mommy." Rose then continued to open the safe. All of the monthly bill-money was inside. She put Portrait in front of the television and told her she'd be right back. Again I came home early from work. Rose had been gone for hours.

After that, night after night Rose was out in the street while I was on my knees praying that she was ok and not laying in some alley, dead. The next morning, she came in. I had decided enough was enough. I was at the door when she came in and I said, "Rose, what's going on with you? I will not accept nothing less than the truth. Night after night I have sat here, hoping and praying that you return home safely and unharmed. There are terrible things happening around here. To get directly to the point, my computer, photography equipment, and radio is missing. Just tell me where it is!"

"Woods, how do you figure I know?"

"Rose, this house has not been burglarized, yet things are missing. I know what the problem is, but I want to hear it from you. Talk to me please, Rose."

"Woods you don't understand, it's all your fault. You stopped loving me. You never notice me anymore so I found a friend that will be there for me. It makes me feel good when I want to feel good. When you wasn't there, it was. Now when it calls me I answer every time. It makes me feel good and it takes away my pain. I love it, I worship it, I even praise it. Woods, I have something very important to tell you."

"What, Rose? What could possibly be more important than this?"

"Woods, I am dying. I have lung cancer."

"No, no, no! Rose, you can't leave me and Portrait! I can't raise her alone."

"Woods, that is not all. I am eight weeks pregnant, but I am not going to have it. I can not bring a drug-addict baby into this world; it won't be right for you or the baby. I made an appointment for an abortion. Woods, would you pay for it?"

"Yes, Rose, I will pay for it. I had been at some low points in my life, but this was the deepest of all. As I sat staring out of my window Portrait came running into the house, crying. I said, "Honey, what's wrong?"

"The kids are laughing at me, they said my mama is an old crack-head."

"Don't cry honey, we are going to be ok!"

"Is she, Daddy? Is mama an old crack-head?"

"Baby, your mama is sick, but she will be ok. She needs us now. Rose, you must give up drugs. The neighborhood is talking and it is embarrassing for Portrait and me."

"Woods how could anyone talk about me? Everybody does it."

"No, not everybody. I don't! Woods, I am dying, anyway. Why not just do it until I die?"

I held Rose. I let her cry on my shoulder and told her that I loved her and that I forgave her. We are not the only people in the world that have gone through ups and downs. I hugged her and kissed her tears away. I had to suffer her pain, just as I had enjoyed her pleasure.

Christmas Eve was supposed to be Rose's last Christmas alive. She was supposed to die sometime during the coming summer. This was a devastating time for me. I was not able to focus properly on anything that mattered. I was to make this Christmas the best ever for me, my wife, and child, just the three of us. We would be shut in for days, enjoying each other. Rose convinced me to let her do the Christmas shopping. She was to ride with her girlfriend to the mall.

I gave her three hundred dollars cash, just thinking this might be something special, even though just months in the past she had forged checks and stolen valuable property from our home for whatever she did with it on the outside of the house long into the night after Rose should have made it home.

Portrait had fallen asleep. Later into the night she woke up, patted me on my shoulder with her little hands. "Daddy, where are my gifts? Where is Mama?"

I knew that something was not right. I looked out my window, thousands of houses out there. She could be in any one of them. I felt that I had to look for her, after all she was my wife and my daughter's mother. Portrait and I went through the neighborhood looking, not knowing where to look, but just looking. Rock cocaine, better known as crack, this controlled substance, is the leading cause of failure of black people today. This substance has set us back years behind our knowledge of pulling forward. It hurts. The average person has no idea what it's like when your spouse becomes dependant on drugs. There is no control – the constant lies, stealing, whatever it takes to fill their need. It's the continuous craving that bring them back, time after time, and making the pusher think, "Why should I work a job when I make more money just standing on a corner?" There were so many places she could be. Portrait and I went from block to block looking for her. We stopped in front of a house that I remembered from the past. I thought it worth a look.

I stopped the car just down from the house. Portrait and I sat there looking at the Christmas decorations: it was beautiful. Then it started to snow, great-looking fluffy snowflakes from out of the darkness. I held Portrait to my chest and said, "Merry Christmas, Portrait."

Then she said, "Merry Christmas. I love you." Then a police car pulled up across the street, put its spot light on us and just sat with its light focusing direct in our face. They never exited their car. I started to wonder, "Do they want me?"

Moments went past, and it started to pull off. The officer then lowered her window, saying to me, "So you are just going to disrespect us and drive off?" There were two officers in the car. A female was driving and a male was on the passenger side. The female officer was doing the talking. "What's your name? Where do you live? What are you doing out here? Whose baby is that? Were you over here buying drugs? Get out of the car. Spread on the front of your car. I think you have drugs on you. Just stay there on the front of your car. We will be there to pat you down and search your car. If we find drugs on you, we are going to call DCFS to take this baby and you are going to jail."

I continued to spread on the front of my car with the spotlight on me. I was starting to cover with snow, but they never exited their car. They were laughing, and seemed to be having fun about my pain.

The spotlight went out and they stopped laughing. She said to me, "Merry Christmas," and pulled off. One week later, I was feeling very down, so I stopped in the neighborhood bar for some very needed unwinding.

I was talking to an old friend. "Gene, it seems everybody knows more about my personal life than I do. Everything that Rose said was a lie."

"Woods, Rose has been coming in here for several years. You know, Woods, me, you, and Rose go a long ways back. Woods, Rose actually laughs and brags about how dumb and stupid you are. Some nights she actually takes the stage about the gags she pulls on you. A week ago, did she tell that she was dying from cancer?"

"Well, yes."

"That is a lie. Rose is not sick and not dying. When she needs money to get her hit, she will say anything, and you will believe her because she is so convincing that you have no other choice. The money that you gave her to have an abortion, she stopped at the corner, sat there for a while with tears rolling down her cheeks, trying to peek around the shadow that was blocking her view. The clinic was to the left and the crack house was to the right. She decided to go right. I don't understand Rose, she seems possessed. She don't give a damn about anything or anyone, not even herself. She only cares about that controlled substance. Tell me, Woods, don't you have a life insurance policy?"

"Well, yes, I do. Why?"

"I think you had better sleep very lightly or probably don't sleep at all. Watch your step."

"Why, what's up?"

"Rose owes a drug dealer so much money and she can't come up with it. Woods, there are plans with your life with your insurance money. Woods, she is very sick. Very sick. When she has your car and is out all night, she is in the back office doing what she does most. Woods, do I need to say more?"

"No you don't."

"She had your car making his deliveries. Every month she gets her public aid, and she owes it out to him."

"Gene, I am getting out of here. I have heard enough." I started home with revenge on my mind. The moment I walked in the door, I grabbed Rose and shelled her to the floor and hit her continuously. I was out of control. My mind was focused only on revenge.

Portrait came running, calling, "Daddy, Daddy, no! Please don't kill my mama! I know she is bad and doing bad things. I know because when you are at work she does bad things and threatens me if I tell you. Daddy, please stop. I love you and Mommy. I want us to be a family."

I grabbed Portrait by her collar and pushed her to the floor. That's when my mind focused together. I jumped up and ran all the way across town to the drug dealer's house. Rose had called him and told him that I was on my way. I stood in his yard shouting very loudly. He came out and threatened me if I didn't leave. I continued to talk, then he and another person came and beat me severely. Both of my eyes were nearly closed from the beating.

As I laid on the ground badly beaten, in severe pain, I looked up and Rose was standing there. I reached up my hand to her and she kicked at me. Then she went to him. They went into the house together and called the police. I was carried to the police station. After twelve hours I was released. It was early in the afternoon and once again I returned to the neighborhood bar with both eyes swollen from the severe beating.

I took it that my friend Gene was not there, so I sat at the bar. When I was having a drink I spilled all of my married problems to the bar tender. His respose was, "Buddy, let me tell you something – drugs cause you those problems. Why don't you let them solve them for you?"

"What do you mean?"

"I have a friend that I want you to meet."

He beeped him, and, a few minutes later, this guy arrived. This guy's whole conversation was about drugs, money and dogging people out. Then he asked me, "Do you want to go into business?"

I said nothing, just looked at him. He said, "Some people can't work the street: they are too soft and ignorant. The street people play them, and there are others that fall victim to their own trap. Just look at me. I was born dirt poor, but now I dress fine every day, drive a fancy car, and all the sex I want. Women will actually kiss your toes for a bump, and men will, too."

He was talking so much and so fast I was looking at him, but my mind was a hundred miles away. I could see the beast in him. He made me an offer to get me started. I had to use my sports car for collateral. After the transaction was made, I went directly home and sat at the kitchen table. I cut up and bagged the product for sale. As the day went on business was good and was picking up more by the days. I got curious about how this substance could control a person's mind, and I tried it continuously, bump after bump. I promised myself that this was the last one.

By then I was out of control and couldn't stop. I realized that if you can control a person's mind, you can control their bodies. What a world, what a world. "World, tell me what has happened to our people. Tell me where is the love that we have lost?"

I wish we had a change of heart, because we can't go on like this. We can't love our brothers – we have lost the love for man. We promise never to be a heartache. Remove the hate and bring love to our hearts. He never thought his people would fail and let his beautiful world become a prison.

"World, let every heart wake up, and let everybody drink from the civil cup. Tell me, world, where is the love that we are missing? Because we can't go on like this. If you can't see it, then we are lost, because hope is just too far away."

All of the hard work of many people is going to sink. Everybody should love everybody, and be concerned. We can't go on like this. We are going down, way down.

We take so much for granted as we go on with our daily lives, seldom considering that the blink of an eye could place us in a situation that will test our matters. When this whole world puts you down, and you feel so all alone, your spirit seems on the ground. You hurt so badly inside until words can't explain the pain. If you go into an eternal sleep, and never awake, that will be ok with you, but you have to come back because there are two little children there depending on me. I wasn't ready to be a parent; how am I going to be a single parent? I am going to do the best I can to the strongest of my ability.

Sometimes it feels like I am going insane. When life itself grabs such a grip on you, all you can do is call the unknown and get to know Him, call out to Him. I didn't forget to pray.

Once again, light started to shine down on me. I was blessed with a great job in a company owned by a great person – Mr. A.G. Flowpack. The position was so flexible, it allowed me to raise my children while I worked. Mr. Flowpack would visit the plant and congratulate the workers for their great work. It would be great to shake his hand and congratulate him, because he has the power to run this company with an iron fist, just as some of the other companies I have worked for before, but that is not his way. Just as I started to rebuild my life, I don't seem to be woman-proof.

I can only hold off from a woman's company for so long. It is not my interest to get into a relationship, to start an addition to my family, seeing that is what my female was interested in. After just a few months into the relationship, things were moving too rapidly. I was not ready to be told "I love you." You and I could not express that word back, so I called off the relationship. I think my mind was too unfocused for this. It was just as bad as when a woman put an unwanted child on a man as it is when a man has uncaring sex with a woman, not caring whether she gets pregnant six months without a relationship. I haven't heard from the person in my first relationship and I learned to cope with reasons.

A Saturday night after the children and I had finished watching a movie, it was then bedtime, there was a banging at my door, and I answered. Niecy was there and she said, "I thought you could use some company."

I paused for a moment, but invited her in.

At the time, I did not think it was appropriate for a woman to ask a man to have sex with them.

"Woods, I made a decision. I have four children and am unwedded since. Since the last time I saw you, I had surgery – I can't get pregnant. It will be a pleasure to get with you and feel you discharge inside of me. So far, you never have and I want you to."

"It's not like I am going to get pregnant. Woods, there is something about you that is really fascinating. I don't want to be the only one of the two of us that feels love for the other, so I am going to disappear out of your life."

Later into the night after the intimacy started, it was at that time that I attempted to get up. Then she put her arms around me and tightly held my body close to hers as darkness then turned to daylight. When the cab arrived, I watched her through my window as it drove away with Niecy in the back seat. I thought to myself this could be the last time I ever see her. A year later, Niecy called and said she had a three-month-old son and asked me when I was coming over to see my child.

I then asked, "What happened to the surgery you were supposed to have had? You promised me there would be no children."

She said, "Yes, I said that, but you seem to be a good father to your children, so I wanted to be a part of that."

It was early fall on a Saturday morning. The sky was overcast with a gentle-falling rain. It was easy to sit all day. I sat around and watched college football on TV or got out and involved with the world. I tried to focus my ex-wife, Rose, out of my mind, but no matter who is at fault to cause a divorce, when it happens it's never an easy thing.

I didn't feel much for driving that day, so I walked to the public transportation to take the train in to the city. Maybe I would get into something that interested me.

It seemed to be a normal train ride. So I decided to put my headphones on and listen to some great music and relax. Even with my headphones on I could still hear my surroundings. In the seat behind me I overheard an attorney deciding their case with another person.

"How can you defend a rape victim when they are now in love with the raper? This young woman was in her home taking a shower. When she finished taking her shower she turned the water off, pulled back the curtain, and this total stranger was standing there, totally nude. He forced himself on her. It started out as rape, then she got involved and started to enjoy it. She still reported it to the police and pressed charges, but changed her mind in court. She said her attacker was sweet, gentle and kind and gave her great pleasure.

Then she said why most women report rape is because the attacker only thinks of themselves. "As soon as they get their pleasure, they don't give a damn about you, but he made sure I was satisfied before he left. Since then, we have bonded a relationship."

I then thought to myself, "Life is such a mystery. It is so hard to just be a righteous person. It seems there is always someone there to set you back, pull you under."

I continued my trouble, noticing the people around me – different personalities with every person. Now I wonder why am I down here. What am I going to do now that I am here? Off on the curb, sitting on the concrete with a big bag beside him, lays a homeless man. Looks as if he spent the night there. I don't know if I am a sucker or just a kind person, but I gave him twenty dollars. I feel for all their pain and sorrow. I don't believe there is much joy that they encounter.

The world doesn't guarantee anyone happiness. It is a major struggle. Why some people count a great success and other people. Today, he knows he is living, but tomorrow is uncertain. I imagine how they feel – just to be loved by someone would mean a great deal. Somewhere deep in my mind, I remembered the positive. It was so great to find a positive life. Where would I be now if a total stranger had not had a heart and took me under his wing that morning when I had no idea what I was up against? Now I am down here reliving a few memories of my past.

I feel I should go have lunch at our favorite little restaurant. I sat in our favorite little corner, dining alone. It was so amazing how fast time goes. I just pictured Brenda in my mind, walking back from the ladies' room, smiling to me all the way back to her seat. Then she would say, "Did you miss me, baby?" I would smile and say, "Yes, darling, I miss you every time I don't see you." It may sound funny, but Brenda, wherever you are at this moment, I still love you. If I could just touch your hand just one more time.

I remember the little tears that formed in her eyes when I told her that I chose Rose. I don't think love like ours will ever end.

After dining alone in the little restaurant, I decided to look in on the little ghetto baby whose mama died on that cold and gray Chicago morning.

Just to enter back into the housing project brought an overcast on my focus, but it was something I felt I had to do. The baby's daddy had been killed two years ago in a rival gang shootout. I was intimidated by the young people gathered out front. My reason for being there was truly innocent – to speak with the people. It is not as bad as the media hypes it up to be, at least from what I see at this point.

There was still a party going on from the night before, to celebrate the release of a high-ranking gang member from prison. How about that?! Whatever happened to celebrating high school and college graduates? This life is a real tangled situation; however, some people can make the best out of any situation and be comfortable.

I was unable to locate the whereabouts of the baby. I felt that I should be out of this area before dark.

Several blocks away there was a gathering of supporters of the family and friends that had lost loved ones to gang violence. I found it not fascinating, but interesting, to hear the brutal ways that their loved ones had been gunned down.

When I entered the room, there was a young woman standing up front speaking out on the behalf of her brother she had lost just months ago. "My brother knew the two young men that ended his life. He grew up with them from childhood. The word was on the street that he was involved in a drug-house robbery that belongs to the neighborhood drug lord."

"When they knocked on the door, he welcomed them in. Just after entering the house, they pulled guns, telling him that he was involved, forcing him to his knees, demanding that he had information of his accomplice. I am sure he had no knowledge of this rival. There was a gun pointed at his head between his eyes, just above his nose. My brother yelled out so loud begging for his life, he was heard through the window outside, pleading, "Don't kill me. I don't know anything about what you are asking me," and then he was shot in that position. If those young men had any idea how they destroyed our family's lives when they shot my brother."

"The only thing they accomplished was another young black man is dead and two more is in jail. If they had any idea of the heart attack that it brought to our family, maybe they would have had a change of heart."

Members of the meeting stood up and hugged each other, discussing issues of the violence they were facing on today's streets.

It was time to head home. At the train station, the homeless man was still hanging around, but this time he approached me with an introduction.

"My name is Marcus Brown, but I'd rather be called 'top cat.' I am not down on my luck; I do ok in life. This is my choice to live like this."

Here is your twenty dollars back. I am a big-city retired police detective. I sit here and observe people. You see, I am a writer. I catch people in their normal acts if they think I am begging and homeless; not like you – you have a heart. I noticed it when I first saw you to the point where I followed you today."

"After three years on the force, I was still just a rookie in experience, but not at heart. I was just not ready for that position, but I was not crazy. There was no police officer that would turn down the chance to become a detective that I know, including myself. My Captain, Jerry Lockheart, had twenty-five years of service. It took him eighteen years to make detective and another seven to make captain."

"His son has been on the force for twelve years and was in line for the next opening for detective. Captain Lockheart let me know that I stole his son's job. Just over a year on the force, my partner and me single-handedly raided an apartment for over a hundred thousand dollars in cash and drugs. The amazing thing about it is that we stumbled and opened the whole thing by accident without an investigation. Whether or not I deserved the promotion or not. I accepted it."

"One year later, Captain Lockheart approached me in the locker room. 'Happy anniversary, hot shot. Congratulations, your training is now over. It is now time for your first major assignment. I guess you thought that you were going to skate right through on you reputation, right, Detective Hot Shot?'"

"'No sir, I just want to do my job to the best of my ability and serve the people of this city.'"

"'Is that the way you feel, Detective Brown?'"

"'Yes, sir, captain. That is right.'"

"'Ok, detective. I will see you in my office after roll call. I have the perfect case for you. My son had twelve years with the force and you walked in with three years and got a lucky break and stole his job. I want you to know, Detective Brown, I don't like you, and I am going to do everything in my power to get you out of here, and he will get the promotion which he deserves.'"

"'Here is your assignment. Either you solve this case or you will die trying.'"

"'Captain, this is absurd. You can't send me down there undercover, alone, under no circumstances. I will go to your superior.'"

"'Let me tell you something right now, my hero. I *am* your superior. I make the decisions in this department and I have assigned you to this case. I need you to work it and there is not a damn thing you can do about it. Get busy now. Get the hell out of my office.'"

"I don't think a law enforcement person should be talked to like that by another."

"I could not just take Captain Lockheart's addresses toward me. I went to his supervisor, but to no advantage. I had my assignment and that was it, going into the deep ghetto of a big city to investigate a murder such as this. I read the police report of the death of Natalie

Johnson, age twenty. Cause of death was determined accidentally. Natalie Johnson was pronounced dead at 3:05 a.m., on the 15th day of September, 1970. No one in Natalie's family believed her death was accidental. They were confident that she was murdered. Natalie was the girlfriend of the area drug lord, street named Ace. The way Natalie died, she was supposed to have been intoxicated with alcohol. She had decided to rest on his water bed. Beside her head was a small electric radio. Then a lit cigarette was in her right hand after she fell asleep. The cigarette fell onto the bed, burning a hole into the water mattress, causing water to get on the radio, electrocuting her, causing her death. The family did not believe that, and neither did I."

"The odds of successfully solving this case were one-thousand-to-one. I would have to have a perfect plan. So far, the only thing I had going for myself was my wise street knowledge. I dressed down to the occasion to fit in the neighborhood. I became close to the family and was allowed to live in as a family member without attracting attention to the street."

"Fifteen-year-old Bunnylee and ten-year-old James were the children of the house. Bunnylee is like the average, normal teenage girl; talking on the phone for hours and causing her mother headaches. James is smart – he reads lots of books daily. A best friend, Robert who is also ten years old, has a mother who is a crack addict."

"Two days later, as I sat in the living room making plans for the case, James and Robert came in. 'What are you up to, Detective Brown?' with a happy, joyful attitude."

"I answered, 'I am just trying to figure out some plans for this case. James, this is supposed to be very confidential – just between the immediately family.'"

"'Robert is down; he knows about everybody in the 'hood and almost everything that is going on, Detective Brown. Let us help you.'"

"'No, no, boys, you just stay out of this. This is not a game. You could get yourselves killed. Furthermore, I could get killed – I am expected to get killed. James, do you know what kind of trouble your mama could get into if the word got out a detective is living in her house, investigating a suspected murder of her daughter, and the suspect is the top drug lord on the South Side? We could all be blown up in a puff of smoke overnight while we sleep. There will be no cooperation from the people of the neighborhood. Ace has the people living in a nutshell of fear.'"

"Ace has made so much money and had so much power, he contributes to the community. He is respected as a high-ranking businessperson in the area. I am going to solve this case, but I have to be careful; Ace is a killer.'"

"'Detective, I am taking a big chance just letting you stay here. The one reason I am doing this is that I want that drug dealer killer off the street.'"

"Robert's mother came for a visit and paid a late respect for her daughter death, and out of the blue, she said, 'I just came from Ace's house and paid him the money. I owed him so I won't end up like so many others that refuse to pay.' Then she said, 'Well, Annie, since you have company, I am going to be leaving. I have a big pot of beef stew cooking back at my house. I need to borrow a few white potatoes. I get my food stamps in two days and I will get you a bag of potatoes.'"

"'Ok, you are welcome. I will get them for you. Thank you.'"

"What is beef stew without potatoes? She was lying through her teeth. She wished that she had a pot of beef stew. She was going to go home and make some fries, and that is all Robert would eat here. But the other little boy, I don't know, probably nothing. I noticed that she was not eating too well. She can't weigh much over a hundred pounds."

"'She thinks that I don't know, but she got her food stamps yesterday. That is how she got the money to pay Ace. She took him all of her food stamps. This Ace, I have to meet him.'"

"'No, that is not a good idea. From now on, everybody call me Top Cat.'"

"'He is never alone, he has guards at all times.'"

"'I believe that, but I still have to meet him.'"

"I slowly walked down the street in front of his house, looking for a few minutes, then turned and walked in the other direction because I needed more information on the person. I stopped slowly and grabbed my forehead and said to myself, 'Maybe James and Robert could help me.'"

"'Ann, I did not meet him, but I have something to ask you.'"

"'Yes, what is it, Top Cat?'"

"'When I got there, I did not know what to do, so I came back. What I need is some inside information. You know I was just thinking James and Robert mentioned that they know about all the people in the area.'"

"'You will not involve these boys. This is a real serious situation. You'd best handle this to your best professional knowledge.'"

"I ok'd her decision, but I wanted to catch up with her friend, Robert's mother. 'What do you think about Robert mother? She could be a help?'"

"'Don't trust her. She is my friend, but she can't be trusted. She will be the one to tell him who you or she is. A crack rock – she will do anything for a hit on the pipe, and tell on you after you have fed her.'"

"'I have the feeling this will get very nasty before it is over. I will walk Robert home.' I knew at that moment, she needed some food and I could help. Just as we approached the door a loud discussion was going on inside. Just for a second, we stood there. Robert used his keys to open the door. The discussion stopped suddenly. She asked, 'What is going on?' in a crying voice. 'Mama, are you all right?'"

"'Yes, Robert. I am fine. It's just that I had baked some potatoes for my boy and the fool ate them. I am tired of this bogus stuff. He is going to get out of here. Tonight he wants to work. Just lay around and eat up everything I bring here for my kid. I know I have a drug problem, and I am sorry – sometimes it gets out of control, but I am a good mother to my children. I let this man move in two years ago and he is still here and has much more of a demand for drugs than I do.'"

"I was careful and asked minimal questions. There was always a chance that someone would find out who I was. After a day I was meeting some of the people in the neighborhood.

I never involved myself with the members of Ace's gang, but there was one who was close to Ace, but had a problem and was scamming from Ace to support his own lifestyle. Just as with many secret films, he was caught on film in the act."

"Early Saturday morning, Ace and his gang took over the park to clean their cars. They used old newspapers to clean their glass just like magic. My camera was pointing right at them, revealing who I was, because I had once made a major drug bust. James and Robert caught wind of it and rushed back to me, but not fast enough. I was kidnapped at the corner store by the person that was scamming Ace."

"He was going to kill me until I told him what I had, and I had more than one copy. He knew Ace would kill him if he found out."

"I was held in a basement, without James and Robert knowing my whereabouts. Those little guys rescued me."

"'Now that I am free, I have to get out of this area.'"

Now to investigate this dangerous situation, although I knew it was a death mission. I handled it with perfection. When I was tied up in that basement, I thought I was going to die. I talked and persuaded those young men not to kill me; if they killed a cop, what would happen to them? I would surely be killed if they told Ace who I was."

"One of the young men wanted to let me go, but the other one was faithful to Ace and refused to do so. As I continued to talk, I was hit and kicked, then they took off to get Ace. That was when I made my narrow escape. I had survived the challenge. I sat watching the late news when it came on: *'a South Side drug lord, known by the street name Ace, was shot and killed outside of his home tonight. He was accused of five murders, but never convicted of any of them.'"*

"I had survived the challenge, but this mission had opened a whole new way of life for me. I had a heart of ice. There was so much money out there in the street. For a short time, I could get in on the action, make a little money and get out. After all, I knew where the spots were. I would just make a few busts and keep the dope for myself and just sell it back to the streets. I would have to get some fellow officer to go along to pull this off."

"I invited several caseworkers over for a Sunday afternoon football game."

"'Marcus, we heard what Captain Lockheart did to you. There was just nothing we could do.'"

"'I know; but you know, fellows, I been thinking something good could come out of this.'"

"'What are you talking about, Marcus?'"

"'I am talking about all of us getting rich. I know how to do it. We work it for a short while and get out. There is so much fast money out there in the streets. It is just a shame to let them make it all.'"

"'Just think about it, Marcus. Do you have any idea what you are getting yourself into, and asking us to be a part of it? Do you know what happens to crooked cops?'"

"The following Sunday, four of five officers returned to finish discussing the issue. The fifth officer called and let us know he was not interested, but promised not to tell. The four of us went on a rampage shaking down dope spots, taking everything they had, turning in just enough to keep us in the clear. I had become so ruthless I had no care in my heart for anyone. Three years into the shake-down, I had made more money than I would have made on my job in ten years."

"Just say they fit a description of a suspect or the car fit the description of a stolen car, when, actually, I should not have pulled them over. I would order them on the ground – sometimes even in mud – and put a gun to the back of their head just to pleasure the evil that had built up inside of me. Take their gold chains and their dope and sell it back to the street. I accepted pay-offs from drug dealers. I could abuse people whenever and how I wanted, and there was nothing they could do about it. I enjoyed doing it, much like when a person is whipping a child. They continue to hit and hit – most times, they are just taking frustrations out on that child for something that upset them earlier."

"Then, one night, it came to me in my sleep. What are you doing? What has come over you? When I awoke, I was a changed person. I put in for a transfer and moved across town. I put together a Little League baseball team, started serving God. I am so ashamed of the person I had become."

"I sat and I tried to fade my mind away from it. No matter how hard I try, the wrong has already been done. How could I make this up to society? Taking advantage of people just because I had the power to do so! I enjoyed making people get on the ground in their nice clothes. I was a sick man. When I look into that young man's eyes… I had the barrel of my gun pressed into his mouth with the clip pulled back. The least little tremble could have put his tonsils through the back of his head. It is bad enough to be a street hustler, but a crooked cop is disgusting. It is so great that our government is enforcing the seatbelt law to save lives, but if our government really wanted to save lives, they would get the illegal drugs and guns off the street."

"When I left town, I was finally wealthy, but money didn't interest me, anymore. I settled in a much smaller town and became an officer there until I retired. Then I began to live like a homeless person – only I am not homeless; I do this to keep my identity. After all of this was over, I took all of my money and built a youth center to direct children in a better way."

"I have now became obsessed with just beating down people just because I had the power to do so; making all that fast money had become addictive."

"The last shakedown I participated in, we busted into a house. It was there and we knew it was. I took a young man, threw him to the floor, put the barrel of my gun into his mouth with the handle pulled back. Just a shake would have put his head down. Looking him directly in the eyes, it looked like something slapped me. I thought, 'This is someone's child. How could I ever become the person that I have?' I let the young man up and yelled out, 'I don't think it is here.'"

"I knew I had to change my life without saying a word to anyone. I quit the police force – just never returning back to work. I moved to another town within days. I was unable to solve the case after a week working down there. I was released from the case, but the damage was done. I had such little concern and respect for our people. Drug lords run the street, and we are afraid to talk. When I was back on regular investigations, just to please myself, I would stop young drivers, especially the ones in their nice cars. I would order them out of the car.

About the Author

I, Elwood Ware was born in 1954 in Yazoo City, Mississippi. I now reside in Harvey, Illinois. I grew up on a cotton plantation doing everything from cotton-picking to gathering pecans. During that time people of color cried out thru prayer for help, wondering if a change will come. It was a challenge, just to get the little help that was available. I was not properly educated. At that time, learning was not a major factor.

I was married in 1983. I have two children from that marriage. I began writing this book in 1984.

I am a single parent, raising my two children, one daughter and one son, in Harvey, Illinois. I devote my time to working a full time job and utilizing my writing skills.